The Conqueror's London

Derek Brechin

SBN 356 02479 2

© London Weekend Television Ltd., 1968
Macdonald & Co. (Publishers) Ltd.

First published in 1968 by
Macdonald & Co. (Publishers) Ltd.
St. Giles House, 49 Poland Street, London W.1

Reprinted 1969
Reprinted August 1969

Made and printed in Great Britain by
Purnell & Sons Ltd., Paulton, Somerset

Discovering London 2

The Conqueror's London

Derek Brechin

MACDONALD : LONDON

Contents

7 The Coming of the English
10 The Decay of the Towns
14 The Spread of Christianity
18 The Danish Invasion
20 King Alfred
22 The Golden Age of Saxon England
26 Saxon London
32 Life in Anglo-Saxon England
43 The Arts in Anglo-Saxon England
48 Anglo-Saxon Architecture
56 Anglo-Saxon and Viking Remains in Museums
59 Norman England
67 Norman London
69 Life in Norman London
89 Norman Remains in Museums
92 Norman Architecture
102 Norman Buildings in London
106 Buildings in London with Norman Remains or Associations
107 A Walk around Smithfield
109 Norman Buildings outside London
110 How to Get There
115 Glossary of Architectural Terms
117 Norman Art
119 Museum List
124 Bibliography

Cover: a detail from the legend of St. Peter at Westminster from a manuscript in The Life of St. Edward the Confessor *in the possession of the Roxburghe Club.*
Slip case illustration: Visscher's Panorama of London 1616 (Guildhall Museum)

Drawings by David Newton

4

Introduction

This book is the second in the series which accompanies the London Weekend Television series *Discovering London*. It deals with the period between the collapse of Roman Britain during the 5th century, and the establishment of a strong centralised government over the whole of England by William the Conqueror and his Normans during the 11th and 12th centuries.

For the first part of this period, the towns were in decay, and there is little mention even of London. But as the country began to become more settled after the Anglo-Saxon invasions and trade was re-established, so the towns were built up again, and London began its steady climb to become the largest and most powerful city in the Kingdom.

Of necessity, much of this book covers the turbulent history of the whole country—brief moments of prosperity broken by wars, raids, and invasions—but it shows how the Londoners gradually began to realise the importance of their city, and how other people all over the country came to accept London's special position.

The Coming of the English

The barbarians force us to the sea, and the sea forces us back to the barbarians.

With these words the British appealed to the Roman emperor in 410 AD for help against Anglo-Saxon invaders. But Rome itself was in danger from the barbarian Goths; the situation which had led to the withdrawal of Roman troops from British soil in the first place was even more desperate and the only help the British received from Rome was advice to organise their own defences.

The very departure of the Romans, however, made this impossible—lack of a central authority led to disunity, to inter-tribal conflict: the Romans gone, potential British leaders, rather than uniting to fight the common enemy, fought against each other. To achieve their personal ends these tribal leaders were even prepared to employ barbarian warriors. According to Gildas, writing about 550, it was just such a move that led to the first Anglo-Saxon settlement in the country.

Till then, and their raids had been going on for some hundred and fifty years, the barbarians had been content with plunder—now land was the prize. A Saxon war-band under Hengist and Horsa, given land in exchange for a promise to defend the south-east (against other barbarians as well as rival British tribes), kept their promise for a while then weighed up the British situation and promptly turned on their employer, seizing Kent for themselves. Thus a barbarian stronghold was established and an example set to other invaders to seize not just plunder, but land.

And land was something the Anglo-Saxons desperately needed. Their own lands were poor and over-populated and they themselves were threatened by the westward move of other peoples, like the Huns. So after the settlement in Kent in 450, the invaders came over in increasing numbers, now bringing their wives and families with them, and gradually settled in Hampshire, Surrey, Essex, and Middlesex. For a time the Britons rallied, first under Ambrosius Aurelius, then under Artorius (probably the original of the legendary King Arthur), but then, once again, after some forty years, disunity and lack of leadership ended the British revival, and the Anglo-Saxons regained the initiative.

The history of the first two hundred years of the Saxon invasions, when not completely obscure, is generally confused. These are the Dark Ages—dark not only in historical outline, but dark too after the brilliance of Roman civilisation. Not until *The Anglo-Saxon Chronicle,* written in the reign of King Alfred, was any attempt made to outline these events which were to transform Britain from a Roman province to an 'English' land with an entirely different way of life—a way of life that was eventually to establish England as a nation with its own distinctive language, society, and government.

Right: *the 5th-century migrations of the Angles and Saxons*

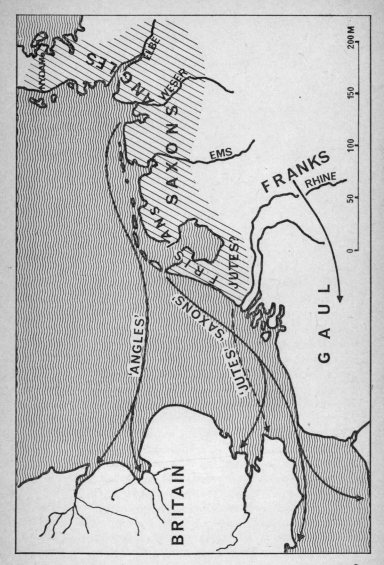

The Decay of the Towns

To the Roman the town was the focal-point of society; the centre of trade and government. To the Saxon the town was an utterly alien thing—especially the Roman town with its huge public buildings, the purpose of which was inconceivable to him. This was the work of giants, something to be feared and avoided. Town life therefore disintegrated and the elaborate buildings fell into decay. Whether any sort of life continued within the towns is difficult to establish—history is silent (even London isn't mentioned in *The Anglo-Saxon Chronicle* between 457 and 604), and, archaeologically, little has come to light. Surviving Britons who did not flee to the West may have squatted amongst the ruins, but it seems unlikely that any sort of organised urban life remained.

By and large, we may say that the decay of the towns (already begun in Roman times) was complete, and that the Roman villa system disappeared, but that there was probably some continuity in agricultural life. The Roman-

British peasant had remained more British than Roman (Christianity, for instance, had scarcely touched him) and there seems no reason why these two pagan agricultural peoples could not have lived harmoniously together. The Saxons penetrated the river valleys and settled on good agricultural ground, building their rude wooden buildings in villages, grouped in large family units.

The ties of kinship (a man's family, in a far wider sense than we use it today) formed a strong element in Anglo-Saxon society. In violent times like these, to have no kin was to be virtually without protection. The system of criminal law they brought with them from Germany (customary to begin with, only later to become written law) was based on the payment of compensation to the kin of the injured party; without kinsfolk a man could offer no deterrent to the potential criminal. The amount of compensation was fixed: each man had his 'wergild', his value reckoned in accordance with his status in society. (Needless to say, in the early days of settlement, there were regional differences—in Kent, for example, a ceorl had a wergild of 2,000 silver pence, in Wessex only 1,000.)

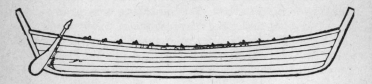

An Anglo-Saxon boat: a long open rowing boat

Anglo-Saxon society was never, even to begin with, a democratic society, and in time the different classes grew further apart, eventually reaching a state of near feudalism even before the Norman Conquest. The reasons for this development are not hard to follow. To begin with, the Saxons believed in an aristocracy. Their society was

11

based on the principle of leadership: a natural belief in time of war. Over and above the ties of kin, then, was the tie binding man to king and to the king's men, the Thegns.

At the bottom of the scale were the unfree, the slaves (amongst whom were many conquered Britons). But it was the man in the middle, the ceorl, the freeman with enough land to support a household, who was the backbone of this graded society. He was the tax-payer and emergency warrior, the worker of the land, and the honour-bound supporter of the lord. Gradually, however, as the kingdom flourished, king and aristocracy grew more prosperous and the status of the ceorl, while not seeming to change in itself, sank by comparison into lesser importance. The habit of the king of rewarding his nobles with rights of taxation meant that the ceorl ceased to pay his taxes direct to the king and now had to pay them to a fellow-subject—thus lowering his own status, and making the latter more powerful.

Over and above this, in an agricultural society such as this was, it only needed an accident of nature or a war, a famine, or a raid, to destroy the ceorl's livelihood, with the result that all he could do in order to survive was hand over his property and himself to a lord, in return for protection and food. Even when disaster didn't ruin the ceorl completely, increased taxation (as for example when money was demanded to buy off the Danes) left him with barely enough to live on, and in order to fulfil his bonds of honour he was obliged to work for his lord instead of paying rent—labour which the lord promptly used to develop and expand his own land. Thus as king and aristocracy grew in importance and wealth, the ceorl's stock sank lower and lower.

This, roughly, was the evolving pattern of society over which the political events of Anglo-Saxon England took place. These may be summarised briefly as the division of the conquered part of England into first seven king-

The Anglo-Saxon cross from the crypt of All Hallows, Berkynge

doms, then three—Northumbria, Mercia, and Wessex—
and finally by the 9th century, one—Wessex. The outstanding event, from the political as well as the religious
point of view, since it helped to systematize English
society, was the conversion of the Saxons to Christianity.

The Spread of Christianity

Christianity in Roman Britain had, as we have said, barely touched the peasant class. It was the religion of the townspeople and its organisation depended on an organised city life. With the decay of the towns, Christianity disappeared from the south and the east, the area conquered by the Saxons. Where it continued to thrive, in the north and west and especially in Ireland, a new Church developed, the Celtic Church, differing in many ways from that of Rome.

But it was from Rome that the first move was made to convert the pagan Saxons. The story goes that Pope Gregory, whose great desire to establish an ecclesiastical empire of all Christian Churches with its capital in Rome brought with it a need to extend the borders of Christendom, first determined on the conversion of England after seeing some Saxon boys in the slave-market in Rome. He asked who these fair-haired blue-eyed boys were, and on being told they were Angles, said: 'Not Angles but Angels.'

Whether this is true or not, the fact is that in 597 a band of monks led by Augustine landed in Kent, instructed by Gregory to reintroduce Christianity to this once Christian country. Kent could hardly have been bettered as a starting-off point. Ten years previously

Ethelbert, King of Kent, had married Berthe, a Frankish princess from Paris, and Berthe was already a Christian, practising her faith in Canterbury. Consequently Ethelbert was prepared to listen to Augustine, albeit in the open air, for fear that indoors he might cast spells.

He then agreed to let Augustine preach in his kingdom, gave him an old Roman church in Canterbury for this purpose, and within a year was himself baptised. Needless to say, on his baptism the nobility followed suit. The Conversion of the English was under way, and under Gregory's guidance, an organised Church was set up, incorporating many aspects of the English paganism in a new guise—'We cannot', wrote Gregory, 'at once deny everything to such rude natures.' Consequently old pagan festivals continued to be celebrated, but now as Christian celebrations—such as the midwinter festival celebrating the beginning of the new year on 25th December, which became Christmas.

The Conversion was by no means an over-night triumph. Too much depended on the influence of the few. To begin with, baptism indicated imitation rather than a sincere change of belief. When, for example, Ethelbert died, his subjects reverted to paganism for the simple reason that the new king had remained a pagan. We shall see too how the bishop sent by Augustine to preach in London fared at the hands of the citizens there—already showing an independence of spirit which was to grow in strength throughout Anglo-Saxon and Norman times.

But paganism was undergoing a two-pronged attack. While Augustine carried the Roman banner in the south, Celtic missionaries were advancing from the north and west. In 634, Oswald, King of Northumbria, already a Christian from his years in exile in Iona, invited Celtic missionaries from there to come and preach in his kingdom. They came, under the leadership of Aidan, and, working from their monastery in Lindisfarne, successfully

15

spread the faith among the people—the people rather than just the nobility.

The Celtic campaign differed from the Roman in this, and it may be that the simple personal approach achieved more in the way of true conversion than the old Roman belief in conversion through imitation of the great. However, once conversion is achieved, organisation is necessary, and this the Celtic Church lacked and the Roman Church possessed.

So, in the long run, it was undoubtedly a good and correct decision made at the Synod of Whitby in 663 that the Celtic Church should accept the authority of Rome and become part of the main body of Christendom. Although the Celtic clergy were, naturally, reluctant to accept this decision, it did resolve a confused situation (the two Churches had, for example, calculated different dates for Easter) and allowed for the organisation of a unified English Church without which a reversion to paganism could easily have taken place.

In time the English Church became one of the strongest and most admired in Christendom, producing not only a long line of missionaries who, such was their pride in their new faith, set about converting the people of their former homeland, Germany, but also a number of scholars and teachers, whose influence on the Arts brought about a cultural achievement far in advance of other nations—literature, both prose and verse, classical and vernacular; sculpture, the beautiful Saxon crosses, some still to be seen today; music, monastic choirs singing double chants; and, perhaps most admired today, the superb hand-painted illuminations of manuscripts and books. Under the impetus of the Church all these flowered and continued to flower until the attacks of the Vikings turned men's minds once again from the arts of peace to the arts of war.

But the arts of peace do not mean merely the product of artists; they include the attainment of law and order,

16

the stability of everyday life, the establishment of a civilised way of life without which, perhaps, the artist cannot flourish. And it is the slow, gradual transformation of English life which, in retrospect, appears the Church's major achievement. It brought to the English a humanity which they had previously lacked; it softened and at the same time strengthened their way of life. The clergy helped govern the country; leading churchmen worked closely with the king, lesser churchmen sat with the king's representatives in the shire-moot. Laws came to be written; customary law was replaced by a codified system.

But over and above the law, the Church's teaching on sin and repentance, its demand for confession and penance, introduced a moral code unheard of by men to whom a crime was something little more than a piece of mischief which if discovered would cost him a fine and then be forgotten. Now a crime was a sin, not just a nuisance to other people, but a stain on himself, and if not confessed and done penance for, a barrier to his entering the kingdom of Heaven.

In this way, in launching an attack on the private conscience, the Church subtly attacked behaviour which could not be punished under the law: drunkenness, the oppression of the poor, the ill-treatment of slaves (it did not condemn slavery; it preferred subtly to encourage an end to it). Gradually, then, the Church sought to eliminate barbarity and inhumanity and replace it with consideration for one's fellow men.

In brief, the Anglo-Saxons had brought with them certain unwritten social ideas of kinship, kingship, law, and order; Christianity, where it didn't transform these ideas completely, softened them and organised them into a working system of written law. By 865 England was by and large a Christian country; but in 865 a great army of Danes invaded.

The Danish Invasion

The Danish force which landed in 865, came to deliver the final blow to an England already reeling from thirty years of attack. In fact, the first landings had come even earlier—*The Anglo-Saxon Chronicle,* compiled in the reign of Alfred the Great, gives 787 as the first recorded arrival of the 'Norsemen'; three ship-loads from the 'Land of Robbers'.

These first raids were, like the Saxons' had been, for plunder rather than land, they were not limited to England, continental harbours too being objects of attack. From 835 the raids became more systematic; every spring the 'heathen men' crossed the North Sea in their long ships, penetrated the east coast rivers, established a safe base, seized horses, and robbed and burned the neighbouring countryside. In 851, a large raiding party anchored in the Thames, and for the first time the Danes wintered in this country. After taking London and Canterbury by storm they encamped on the Isle of Thanet.

At this time England was not yet a united kingdom. Hence there was no central control to organise defences against the invaders. Northumbria, East Anglia, and Mercia soon fell, and their kings fled or were slain. Monasteries and libraries were burned to the ground. After the all-out attack of 865 only one English kingdom remained unravaged—Wessex.

Under Egbert (802–839) the kingdom of Wessex gained supremacy over the rest of England. Egbert became 'Bretwalda', the name given by Bede to kings whose overlordship was recognised by other royal houses. It means, roughly, ruler of Britain, a title lacking in accuracy, but of interest in that it shows, through acceptance of the idea of one king having authority over others, that England was beginning to be regarded as an entity.

The role of 'king', and the importance of having a strong person in that role will be examined later on; for the moment it is enough to say that the royal house of Wessex became ultimately the royal house of the Kingdom of England largely because it produced in succession a number of great kings—and none greater than Alfred.

A Viking tombstone which is now in the Guildhall Museum

King Alfred

Alfred came to the throne in 871, a year which saw eight major battles against the Danes. He rallied the English and successfully held out till the end of the year. But finally, hopelessly outnumbered (a large part of his army, composed mainly of farmers, left the field of battle to go and tend their own fields and pastures), Alfred could only buy peace by paying tribute—'danegeld' as it was called.

He used the time to organise, and in 876 defeated the Danes at Wareham. But in 877 he himself was defeated and forced to retire to Athelney (where, the story goes, he was even defeated by some cakes!). But again he used the time well, and shortly after Easter, according to plan, he joined his united forces at a secret rendezvous, and, taking the enemy by surprise, utterly defeated them at Eddington.

Alfred, however, wanted more than victory; he wanted peace. He invited the defeated Danish king to be baptised as a Christian, and himself acted as god-father. The way was paved towards peaceful co-existence between English and Dane. But not immediately. The Treaty of Wedmore, although it brought peace with the conquered Danes, did not prevent new Danish armies from attacking the country. Alfred realised this, and again he set about organising the English forces.

An example of Anglo-Saxon pottery

He kept his army in training, and to avoid a repeat of his peasant soldiers' returning to their farms in mid-battle he divided the 'fyrd', the call-up, into two halves, each taking it in turn to fight and farm. 'The Father of the Navy,' he built a fleet of ships, hoping to prevent the Danes from landing. The most original and effective of his military reforms was the creation of fortified towns, which he peopled with proven fighting men. In his one non-defensive move he seized London from the Danes, in whose hands it had been left under the Treaty of Wedmore. Yet, even in this, his prime motive was probably defence.

If he had not realised it already, the impression the capture of the city made on the rest of England outside Wessex must have made him realise that London was the key, not only to effective defence against the Danes, but to the creation of a completely united kingdom of England. Alfred strengthened the walls of the city, but did not retain immediate control of it for himself. He gave it instead to the ruler of English Mercia—again an act which could only foster unity amongst the English.

The Golden Age of Saxon England

Alfred died in 901 AD and his son, Edward the Elder, and grandson, Athelstan, continued his work of reconquering the areas still occupied by the Danes, a task made easier by the idea of unity inspired by Alfred's leadership. The Danes were not driven out, but forced to accept the English king as overlord. And English king in every sense Athelstan was—his territory stretched from the English Channel to the River Clyde.

England was at last a united kingdom. Trade began to flourish again, largely due to the Danes, who were great traders and lovers of travel, especially by sea. It helped that there were now fellow Northmen established in maritime countries throughout Europe (such as Normandy) and beyond, to provide new markets for English exports.

Under Edgar the Peaceful (959-975) England was at the height of its new prosperity, and with this prosperity and peace, came a great revival of the monasteries,

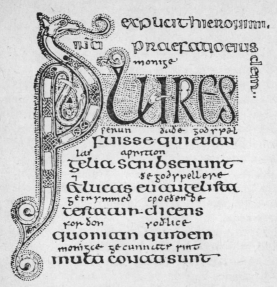

Part of an Anglo-Saxon illuminated manuscript

almost completely wiped out by the Danish invasions. With this revival, inspired by St. Dunstan, Abbot of Glastonbury, came a new flowering of the arts and an immense enthusiasm for learning which would have gladdened the heart of Alfred, that great man of peace as well as war, who, by personal example, had encouraged men to aim at higher standards of culture by means of knowledge and religion.

But this, the golden age of Saxon England, did not last for long. As we have said, the role of king at this time demanded a strong personality; peace and unity depended ultimately on the ability of the king to maintain control. In 978 Ethelred the Unready (actually the 'Redeless', perhaps better translated as 'lacking in counsel') came to the throne, and under his weak and inconsistent rule united England fell apart.

23

As soon as this became obvious, the Danes once again directed their boats at the English shore and a new wave of invasions was under way. The best Ethelred could do was attempt to buy them off. They returned for more. Then Ethelred, such was his weakness and stupidity, ordered a massacre of the Danes already living in the country—his own subjects. As a result, the King of Denmark, Sweyn Forkbeard, attacked with new determination. Ethelred fled to Normandy, leaving England in Danish hands. At first only the citizens of London offered any resistance, successfully staving off attack. Then, both kings having died, their sons fought on till finally Edmund Ironside died and the Danish King Canute was accepted as King of England as well.

Canute reigned from 1016 to 1035, and under his rule England prospered again. Canute, already a Christian, promised to govern by the laws of King Edgar, and he kept his promise. He rebuilt the churches and abbeys which the Danes had destroyed; he made new laws with no distinction between Dane and Englishman; he ruled as a native king and he ruled strongly and well. The one weakness in his otherwise successful reign was that too much power was allowed to pass to the great earls of the kingdom. After his death Canute's empire (which by this time also included Norway) fell to pieces. He was succeeded briefly in turn by his two sons, after which the old royal line was restored with Ethelred's son, Edward, later known as 'The Confessor'.

Edward was not the king England required at this time. He was not without ability, but his temperament was not that of a strong ruler who could contain the growing power of the earls. Indeed, he more or less allowed himself to be ruled by one of them: Earl Godwin of Wessex, whose daughter he married and whose son, Harold, destined to succeed on Edward's death, virtually took over the running of the country in the last years of Edward's life while he busied himself with a project dearer to his heart—the foundation of a church to St. Peter in Westminster.

On Edward's death three men sought the throne of England—Harold of Wessex, Harold Hardrada, King of Norway, and William, Duke of Normandy, who claimed that Edward had promised him the throne and further claimed that Harold of Wessex had sworn an oath to be his man and help him become King of England. If Edward had indeed made the promise he had no right to do so: accession to the throne depended on gaining the assent of the great men of the country. This assent Harold of Wessex received and was duly crowned. William made preparations for invasion; Harold prepared to meet him.

But then, luckily for William, unluckily for Harold, the Norwegians invaded just before the Norman landing. Harold was forced to march north, and although he won a quick decisive victory at Stamford Bridge, near York, it's likely that his resources were weakened for the forthcoming battle with William. He might have done well to delay the meeting, but for some reason, probably elation over his triumph against the Norwegians, he elected to tackle the Normans as quickly as possible.

It was an unfortunate decision—the English were no match for the Norman cavalry and archers; Harold himself was killed. William's victory at Hastings was decisive. He marched north towards London, devastating the country on the way. He did not, however, immediately attack London. He contented himself with burning Southwark and retiring to Berkhampstead, where he remained in a threatening position until the Londoners were forced to submit. This they finally did and William was crowned in Westminster Abbey on Christmas Day, 1066. For the last time in our history, as it turned out, this country had been invaded and conquered. Saxon England had become Norman England.

Saxon London

It seems likely that with the general decay of the towns in the first two centuries of Saxon occupation London ceased to exist as a city.

Before 600 AD we hear of it only once, in 456, when, after the Battle of Crayford in Kent, the defeated Britons fled back to London. This presumably was a London army, which would indicate that Roman-Britons were still living in the city, but it seems doubtful that they were leading any sort of organised urban existence. London's vitality arises from her position of importance as a centre for trade with the continent, trade requires security and freedom of movement in order to flourish; these requirements were lacking at this time.

Thus it seems unlikely that London survived, except as an uneasy home for the Roman-Britons squatting amongst the ruins of her crumbling buildings. In time many of these probably slipped away to the uncon-quered mountainous areas in the west, joining their

The seal of King Edward the Confessor

Christian fellows surviving there. Neglect changed the face of London: the Walbrook conduit became choked through lack of care, and the water, unable to escape, formed a marshy area to the north of the walls which became known in medieval times as Moorfields.

The next mention we have of London is in 604, seven years after the landing of St. Augustine, but it seems likely that during the 6th century as the south-east became more settled generally, London began to recover something of its former vitality. But Saxon London did not grow up on the foundations of Roman London. As we have seen, the Saxons feared and hated cities, and London, by its sheer size was doubtless the most fearsome of all. Consequently, they avoided the city itself, preferring to settle in the wooded country round about it—in Kensington, Paddington, Islington, on the south bank of the Thames, and in Essex in the valley of the Roding.

Later, the more daring moved into the city itself, and

their wooden buildings appeared alongside the stone ruins of Roman London. Saxon remains from the late 6th century have been found there, and it seems clear that by 604, the year in which Augustine sent Bishop Mellitus to establish a bishopric in London, there was quite a large population. Or, if not large, at least single-minded in their determination to remain pagan. Either way, they threw Bishop Mellitus out.

Mellitus fled to Gaul, deserting the church which he had built in honour of St. Paul—the first church on the site of what is now St. Paul's Cathedral.

Bishop Cedd restored the Christian faith to London in the 650s, and some thirty years later Bishop Erkenwald, as well as building London's north gate—Bishopsgate—and founding the Abbeys of Barking and Chertsey, rebuilt St. Paul's in stone, where it stood till the Vikings burned it down in the 9th century. Raised again in 962, destroyed by fire in 1087, it was rebuilt and enlarged by the Normans and survived (with alterations and extensions) till the Great Fire in 1666, after which the present magnificent building was created by Sir Christopher Wren.

By the 670s, London was firmly Christianised (the first Westminster Abbey was also in existence—see Legend of Westminster Abbey) but its initial reluctance meant that Canterbury and not London, as planned by Pope Gregory, became the centre of Christianity in England. London's importance remained, as it had been in Roman times, as a centre of trade. The more settled conditions allowed trade to flourish again, and by 730 Bede was referring to it as 'the mart of many nations by land and sea'. 754 saw the establishment of the first regular tariff on goods brought into the Port of London. The steady growth in prosperity continued, despite a series of fires, until the conditions of peace and security vital to trade vanished with the coming of the Danes.

The Danes from the first used the Thames as a way of

penetrating into the heart of the country; London, by its bridge, commanded the river so it was an object of continual attack. The military importance of London became clear for the first time. We have seen how Alfred's recapture of the city made a great impression on the rest of the country; the realisation of the importance of their city had an equally great effect on the Londoners.

It is here perhaps that we see for the first time that pride in their city and independence of spirit that was to set Londoners apart from the general movements of society throughout the ensuing centuries.

In the meantime, however, the immediate aim was to hold it against the Danes. It had fallen into their hands several times before Alfred gained control, fortified the city, and strengthened its walls (a picture can be seen on the walls of the Royal Exchange illustrating this). The Danes were successfully repulsed, and during the long lull in the invasions caused by a struggle for supremacy in their homelands and the strong rule of Alfred and his successors in this country, London began to busy itself with trade again.

Then, under the weak rule of Ethelred, the invasions began again, with London more of a target than ever. That they succeeded in beating off the Danish attacks for so long is a tribute to the efforts of the Londoners themselves who sustained the fight with little or no assistance from the forces of the king. Control of London Bridge was the main objective; at one point, while it was still in Saxon hands, the Danes attempted to by-pass it by digging a canal round the southern end in order to get their ships through. On another occasion, when the bridge was in Danish hands, Ethelbert's forces threw hawsers round the piers of the bridge and dragged them down. 'London Bridge Is Falling Down' goes the old song, and here we see just how old it might be.

Despite their efforts, however, the Londoners were finally forced to submit to Sweyn, the Danish king. After a year Sweyn died, and two years later, in 1016, Ethelred died. Sweyn's son, Canute, claimed the throne and was acknowledged as king everywhere except in London. The Londoners elected Ethelred's son, Edmund. With their support, Edmund continued the fight against Canute, but within seven months Edmund too was dead, and Canute was accepted as king. London became a Danish city.

This, as it turned out, was no great tragedy for the city; in fact, it proved a shot in the arm to its trading activities. As we have said, the Danes were great traders, whose far-reaching contacts brought new markets for foreign trade. Dane and Saxon, not after all so different in race and origin, settled down together within the city.

The newcomers too established communities on the outskirts—Tooley Street, in Southwark, bears witness of one such Danish quarter. St. Olaf (whence 'Tooley') is commemorated too within the city in the Church of St. Olave, in Hart Street. Aldwych is a Danish name, but in this case the name was only given to it in modern times in the knowledge that it had once been a Danish settlement—at the heart of which stood a church, whose replacement is now known to us, for this reason, as St. Clement Danes. The government of London was greatly influenced by Danish law—the 'Husting', the court at which the Lord Mayor is elected derives from the 'house assembly' which was meeting weekly from the end of the 10th century to deal with commercial and civil business.

In 1042, the Saxon line was restored in Edward the Confessor, whose major contribution to the story of London was the building of his Palace of Westminster, and nearby, the new Westminster Abbey. These will be described in detail elsewhere; the immediate significance to London lay in the fact that a royal residence had been built there. By this time, London was far and away the largest and in many ways the most important town in England, but it was not the capital.

This role was filled by Winchester, if only because the once-mobile treasury had found a permanent home there. There too the early Saxon kings were buried (their graves—including that of Canute—can be seen in chests on a screen round the chancel in Winchester Cathedral) but to call it a capital city in any modern sense would be misleading. As long as the king's court remained mobile there was no need for, or any thought of, a capital city. The significance of Edward's Palace, then, is the creation of a permanent royal home, and in a city whose size and growing political awareness made it well qualified to become the national capital. This, of course, did not take place till much later when once again its geographical position proved of major importance, providing a suitable base for kings whose territory included lands in France as well as England.

By the time of the Norman Conquest, London was already a city with a mind of its own; it possessed a certain amount of self-government; it had gained liberties and privileges (mainly in commerce) which future kings would be forced to treat with respect. Indeed it was soon to proclaim its right to take part in the election of the king himself. In its sense of its own importance as well as in the eyes of others London was moving towards its position as capital city.

A Danish drinking horn

Life in Anglo-Saxon England

Anglo-Saxon Government

The corner-stone of government in Saxon society was the king. Although there were certain reins on his power controlled by the Witan (in full, Witenagemot; a council of 'wise men' chosen from the aristocracy), this council should not be seen as any sort of democratic parliament. True, it was responsible for the election of the king—qualification for kingship rested upon membership of the royal family and the Witan chose from within that membership the most suitable successor, not necessarily the son of the previous king—and it also advised him on matters of government, but in the long run the king, once elected, was free to act much as he chose.

Successful rule, then, depended greatly on the personality of the king, who, to begin with, had no fixed court but travelled around with his followers, mainly in order to collect his rents, which, being paid in food, had to be eaten on the spot. A king of no fixed abode, he could summon his Witan when he required it (to approve new laws, for example) to whichever royal estate he happened to be occupying at the time.

Later, as kingdoms became bigger, royal representatives were created to administer local justice. These, the ealdormen (from whom come the aldermen in present-day local politics), attended and supervised the meetings of the local court and the process whereby the handling of regional affairs passed from the freemen to the king, was under way.

The residence of an Anglo-Saxon nobleman. This illustration is taken from a contemporary manuscript.

By the time of the Norman Conquest this process was so complete and efficient for royal purposes that William made little attempt to change it, so well did it strengthen his hold on the country as a whole and enable him to establish a firm feudal superstructure on society.

The old popular assemblies remained in existence—the 'hundred' (most likely, to begin with at any rate, meetings of groups of a hundred families); above this, the 'shire-moot'; and above this still, the 'folk-moot'—but these 'moots', or courts, were now controlled by the king's officers. The shire-reeve (the origin of the present-day sheriff) was one of the most vital figures in the system, personifying royal authority to lord and peasant alike, delivering the king's writ and ensuring his wishes were carried out in the area.

This process of change in local government was a slow gradual one, only clearing in outline in the 10th and 11th centuries, when the Danish invasions undoubtedly added impetus to it, hastening the development of this near-fuedal state by forcing the poor into the hands of the lord. In addition, many of the institutions of government were most likely Danish innovations. We have already noted the 'husting'; it may be that the 'hundred' (in Danish areas, the 'wapentake') was likewise a Danish introduction, or at least a refinement of an earlier Saxon idea.

In London, by the end of the Saxon period, local government was much more complex, with a larger number of courts, one for each of the wards into which the city had been divided. There were also the 'sokes', privileged areas which came under private jurisdiction. But public authority was the general rule, and the court of highest authority remained the folk-moot, which met three times a year, attended by every citizen (in theory at least), in the open air on the highest ground in the city—beside St. Paul's Cathedral.

Law and Order

We have already mentioned the Saxon law of compensation to the injured party by payment of his 'wergild' to his kinsfolk. Some crimes of course were considered beyond compensation—witchcraft, arson, and predictably, treachery to one's lord or king. The punishment for these was hanging. But in crimes of the first category it was legal for the kindred to refuse payment of the wergild and take revenge into their own hands. This meant of course retaliation by the kindred of the original criminal, and the blood feud thus embarked on could continue for many years.

Later kings tried to stamp out this practice with its inherent danger that a kindred might grow too powerful and set itself above the law. But passing laws is one thing, ensuring they are observed is another, especially in an age where a police force such as we know it was non-existent. Maintenance of law and order was in the hands of the people themselves. That it worked at all shows the genius for co-operation that the Saxons possessed. When a crime was committed there followed a 'hue and cry'—all freemen were called out to pursue and catch the criminal (rather like the 'Posse' we're all familiar with from Western films).

Once captured, the criminal was brought to trial—a trial which bore little resemblance to the court procedure of today. It was in fact a Trial by Ordeal, provided, that is, the accused failed to get through the early stages which consisted of swearing an oath—'By the Lord, I am not guilty of act or part in the crime with which I am charged'—backed by his 'oath-helpers' who swore, 'By the Lord, the defendant's oath is true and not false'. This was preceded by an oath made by the accuser, swearing that he was justified in bringing the charge. If this was successful and the defendant's was not, the Trial by Ordeal commenced.

In the ordeal by fire, the accused took a bar of red-hot iron in his hand and walked for a fixed distance, or he walked over red-hot ploughshares set unequally apart. In the ordeal by water, he plunged his hand into boiling water to draw out a stone. The part affected was wrapped in linen (in Christian times by a priest), and if on removal after three days the wound had healed, the accused was found not guilty; if it had festered he was convicted. The idea behind the Ordeal was that heaven might intervene and pass judgement.

Maintenance of law and order remained for a long time the task of the people themselves, co-operative but unorganised. The first appearance of anything resembling a police force seems to have been made in London in the early 10th century where a peace-gild was formed. Composed of groups of ten men, combining to form groups of one hundred under a headman, its aim was not only to create more organised action against criminals, but also to make available out of the common property of the gild money to compensate the injured party. A police 'force', then, but it remained a voluntary organisation run by the people, not a state-run institution.

Saxon Boats and Armour

The boats in which the Saxons arrived in our country were little more than long open rowing boats, made out of oak planks stretching the full length of the vessel. The oars were worked over the sides and the rowlocks were so shaped that the boat could not be backed. It was steered by paddle and tiller in the stern. There was no mast and no sail, and the voyage must have been hazardous to say the least.

The Saxons' chief weapons were the spear (wooden with iron head), the axe, and the dagger or 'scramasax' (from which we get the name Sax-on). For defence they carried shields, round and made of wood, the metal boss in the centre often spiked for use as a weapon at close quarters. The weapons of the wealthier were often richly decorated. The wealthy too would have worn a mail tunic or 'byrnie' of interlocking rings; the poorer Saxon's byrnie was of leather. Helmets were sometimes conical, but more often of Phrygian shape.

An Anglo-Saxon warrior carrying a sword and circular shield

Danish Boats and Armour

Danish boats were a definite advance on Saxon ones. Still long, built of oak, and surprisingly shallow, they were nonetheless infinitely more seaworthy and comfortable.

They were rowed (the oars going through rather than over the sides) but had in addition mast and sail. They rose high at stern and prow, carved to resemble dragons. Their boats were a source of great pride to the Danes and they were often given poetical names.

Their principal weapons were the sword, the spear, and the battle-axe, frequently engraved and decorated. Their tunics were thick, made of leather and covered with interlocking iron rings. The Viking helmet is well-known—a close-fitting metal cap adorned with horns.

Anglo-Saxon Dress

Saxon clothing was simple and serviceable, the men wearing a woollen shirt or tunic (the fore-runner of the medieval smock), long woollen trousers and thick stockings. When working out of doors they wore skin or leather garments, sometimes fur or leather tunics with heavy cloaks fastened by buckles, fur caps and gloves, leather belts, and shoes.

Women too used woollen clothing, wearing a long, loose tunic which reached to their feet, over a linen undergarment, and over this a coat with wide sleeves. The head was covered with a silk or linen wrap.

Both men and women were vain and passionately fond of bracelets, brooches, rings, and necklaces of bronze, gold, and amber. But these, needless to say, were in the possession only of the rich, upper class. The basic pattern of their clothing was similar to that of the peasant, but of better materials.

Both sexes wore their hair long, and took great care of their appearance. Even the warrior setting off to battle made sure he was as splendidly arrayed as possible.

Vanity and personal cleanliness require an assortment of toilet articles, and many of these have been found by archaeologists—bone combs, silver tweezers, and toothpicks, bronze scissors and nail-cleaners.

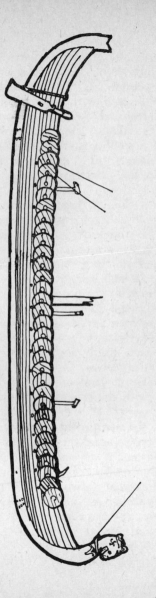

A Viking ship. This was far more advanced than the Anglo-Saxon ship shown on page 11. Although still open, its sides were higher and the oars went through them instead of through rowlocks over the top. It was fitted with sails, and the stern and prow were richly carved.

Dwellings

To begin with, as we have seen, the Saxons were country dwellers. They settled in families, or groups of families, and these settlements were named after the family names—Paddington was the dwelling place of the Paddings. 'Ton', from which the word 'town' derives, meant a large farm or village. 'Ham', our modern word 'Home', represented a smaller settlement. It's a fair assumption that place names today ending in -ton or -ham are of Saxon origin, as indeed are those containing 'wick', 'ley', or 'den', 'hurst', 'fold', or 'field'.

The settlers cleared themselves an area and built their homes close together for protection. These homes were modest, to say the least. Not surprisingly, since built of wood at best, straw and mud at worst, few traces remain of these, but from those we have, it would seem that the unfree lived in little more than hovels, sometimes partly sunk into the ground; the ceorls in somewhat more substantial buildings, made of daub and wattle over a timber framework and probably thatched. In these the family frequently shared their accommodation with their animals, not necessarily domestic, with only a low wall or screen separating them.

Even the Great Hall of the Chief was great only in comparison with the other buildings. Bigger it certainly was, but it was still little more than a glorified barn, with a log fire in the centre (the chimney being a hole in the ceiling), weapons hung on the walls, and sleeping areas along the sides. Privacy was a virtual impossibility, the one large room being shared by the chief and his followers and servants alike. Even the halls of kings resembled this for many years; probably not until the time of Alfred were any built in stone.

Domestic Life

Furnishing was of the simplest—wooden trestle-type tables and wooden benches for both seating and sleeping purposes.

For eating, only a knife was used, each person carrying his own; spoons and forks were virtually non-existent.

Saxon table glass was extremely beautiful and very colourful, never clear white, but amber, blue, or green, and decorated with 'tears' of the molten glass, incredibly contrived so that the wine in the glass could flow into them. Pottery was used by the lower classes in place of glass, generally hand-made until the 8th century when wheel-turned pottery became the rule. Wooden platters and horns for drinking were probably the utensils used by the majority.

Food in the small enclosed world of the largely self-subsisting village was probably rather unexciting, a somewhat repetitive menu of poorly cooked meals. It has been suggested that drunkenness—a great Saxon pastime—may be attributed to the need for ale or mead to cover the taste of the food.

In the towns, however, especially market towns like London, a brighter fare must have been offered. By the 9th century London was probably the home of many cookshops and inns. These sprang up because of the lack of adequate cooking equipment in the average home. Ovens, and the fuel to burn in them, were expensive and hard to come by. Not only that, but in homes built of timber and thatch they were obviously a fire hazard.

In addition, about a third of the population was probably itinerant and ready customers for the cookshop. The service it provided was generally a 'take-away' one, rather like that of a modern fish and chip shop. But the Saxon Londoner could also take his food to the shop and have it cooked. By and large, then, apart from the richer household with its own oven, the average family pur-

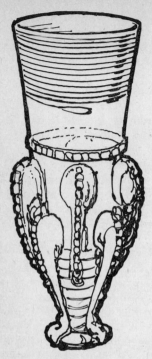

A very fine example of Anglo-Saxon glass. Shows the intricate work which their craftsmen were capable of.

chased ready cooked meals adding to them vegetables that could be easily prepared indoors. The menus of the various classes would have been rather similar, varying only in the cut of meat they could afford to buy.

Saxon London provided much of its foodstuff from its own city gardens, but by the 9th century it was too large to be entirely self-sufficient and produce was brought in from farms in the Thames Valley and elsewhere. A Saxon farm was found underneath the Treasury building in Whitehall.

Whether shops existed in London by this time is not known, but it seems likely. Smaller produce was probably taken round by cart and cried through the streets.

The Arts in Anglo-Saxon England

Anglo-Saxon Art and Design

We have noted in the Saxon dress their love of ornament—such as bracelets, brooches, and necklets. These
were the works of art of the early settlement. The craftsmanship was astonishing by any standards; even more so
when contrasted with their primitive achievements in
building. It's possible that this unexpected taste for, and
ability to create, exquisite pieces of jewellery, may have
been caused by contact with the culture of the Goths in
South Russia during the Saxons' earlier travels before
settling in this country.

Examples of Saxon jewellery can be seen in the Guildhall Museum (a hoard of jewellery found in Cheapside,
rings, brooches, ear-rings, mostly made of pewter) and in
the London Museum (a ring and bracelet, both found in
London, which therefore indicates a later date for them);
but the greatest collection is undoubtedly the Sutton Hoo
Treasure, to be seen in the King Edward VII Gallery of
the British Museum.

In 1939 this, perhaps the greatest single find made by British archaeologists, was dug up at Sutton Hoo, on the Suffolk coast, about 10 miles from Ipswich. Beneath a mound of earth, or 'barrow' (the Saxon method of burial), was found the remains of a complete Saxon ship. In the centre of the ship there was what may be called a 'mini-barrow'—a smaller mound of earth covering a wooden cabin, inside which were the personal effects of the Saxon chief (probably King Ethelhere of East Anglia, killed in 655), in whose honour the ship had been ceremoniously carried inland and buried.

There is no space here to list all the objects which go to make up this treasure. Suffice it to say that, as well as weapons (including a gold-encrusted sword), bronze and silver bowls, and drinking horns, there is an incredible profusion of jewellery. There are gold pieces set with garnets, mosaic glass, and filagree, but, outstanding amongst the superb goldsmiths' work is a purse with an exquisitely ornamented lid, whose hinges and catch still work perfectly after thirteen hundred years. All in all, a collection which demonstrates clearly what the early Saxon artist was capable of.

The purse lid from the Sutton Hoo treasure in the British Museum

Danish Art

Danish art does not reveal the same taste as Saxon. Their ideas were original but uncontrolled, their brooches for example over-ornamented to the extent of grotesqueness. Their furniture, like their ships, was richly decorated and extravagantly carved.

Literature

In the earliest Saxon period, literature, as such, cannot be said to have existed. But the Saxons brought with them a tradition of story-telling and spoken verse which later came to be written down. The best-known Saxon poem is *Beowulf*, the story of a warrior slaying a dragon which had plagued the royal court, but also, and more important from a historical point of view, the source of much of our knowledge of Saxon society and customs. First written down in the late 9th century, the precious manuscript is now kept in the British Museum, in Case S of the Manuscript Room.

This room also contains many other exceptional Saxon documents, charters, and many beautiful illuminated manuscripts.

The Saxon artist's love of colour and design had found a new outlet with the coming of Christianity in the illustration and illumination of religious works. This new art was notable for the richness of its designs, especially in the decoration of initials, for its clear round lettering, and for the brilliance of its colours. One of the best examples can be seen in the Magna Carta Room of the British Museum. This, the Lindisfarne Gospels, is believed to have been written about 700, by Eadfrith, the Bishop of Lindisfarne.

The Venerable Bede (673–735), was the first outstanding figure in English literature. A scholarly writer, drawing his style from the fine collection of classical and religious works available in the monastery at Jarrow where he spent almost his entire life, he was also blessed with a sense of history. Of all his books his *Ecclesiastical History of the English Nation* is the most important. The late 8th-century manuscript of this is one of the outstanding exhibits of the Manuscript Room.

Another is an 11th-century copy of *The Anglo-Saxon Chronicle*, a record of the important events of the age which successive generations of monks continued until the middle of the 12th century from its beginning in the 9th, probably at the instigation of Alfred the Great.

This astonishing man, whom we have already seen as an inspiring and imaginative military leader, sought more for himself and his people than victory over the Danes; he wanted victory over ignorance and barbarism. The achievements of Bede and his contemporaries had been virtually erased by the long struggle against the Danes. In Alfred's own words: '... So utterly has knowledge fallen away in England that when I began to rule there were very few men ...who could understand their Mass-Books and Offices in English, or even translate a letter from Latin into English.'

Bede and his fellow monks had written largely in Latin; even this ability had been all but lost. But the bulk of the population spoke English, and Alfred wanted education to be general, not just for the few. Consequently, what was needed was the study of Latin texts for the knowledge, learning, and example they contained, and, equally important, the translation of these texts into the native tongue to encourage a genuine English culture.

Alfred undertook this task himself. At the age of forty, in the middle of the Danish wars, he began to learn Latin. At the same time, he organised schools for 'all the free youth of England'. And while these were learning to read their own language, Alfred began the task of translating classical works into that language; at first with the help of scholars, later, as his own ability increased, taking more and more of a hand in the translations himself, adding to them passages of his own.

The books translated contained philosophical and religious works, but Alfred laid special emphasis on history. Among the historical works translated was Bede's *Ecclesiastical History*. Out of the study of past events came the desire to record contemporary events as they happened, *The Anglo-Saxon Chronicle* was begun; English history was brought up to date (Alfred himself most likely writing about his wars with the Danes) and the record was kept up by monastic chroniclers in later years. Written in English it laid the foundations of a national prose literature.

Alfred wrote: 'It has always been my desire to live worthily, and after my death to leave a memory of good works to posterity.'

Few men can have attained their desire so completely; few men have so completely deserved the description 'Great'.

Anglo-Saxon Architecture

Timber was the natural building material to the Saxons, coming as they did from the forested areas of Northern Europe. When, later, they came to build in stone, their constructions were simple and crude, often revealing an attempt to do with stone what they were used to doing with wood. Their difficulty in adapting to stone-work can be seen in the way they tackled corners, where the stones were made to alternate vertically and horizontally, an arrangement which does not offer great strength (an example of this can be seen in the tower of St. Michael's Church in Oxford). There was little thought of balance within the building, nave and chancel being allotted separate and disproportionate areas. Windows and doors were no more than small holes in the walls, topped by a small arch or a triangle of stones.

Practically no Saxon building survives in London, devastated as it was by so many fires. However, the apse of a Saxon church can be seen in the crypt of St. Bride's in Fleet Street, and also in the crypt of All Hallows Berkynge by the Tower, founded as early as 675, where parts of an 11th-century Saxon cross have also been found.

To see Saxon construction in a more complete form one has to go further afield—to Bradford-on-Avon, to St. Martin's in Canterbury, or St. Peter's in Bradwell, Essex.

But there is, near Ongar, which is on the Central Line of the Underground, a little church at Greensted where one can see a Saxon nave, made of wood, the structure being simply of upright tree-trunks split in half.

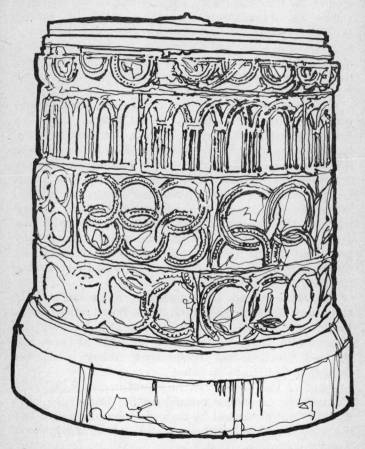

The font from St. Martin's, Canterbury: the lower part is a good example of Anglo-Saxon decoration, and the upper half with the arches is Norman.

The Legend of the Founding of Westminster Abbey

Tradition has it that in 616 a church was built by the king of the East Saxons on Thorney Island, the area now known as Westminster, and consecrated by Bishop Mellitus. No traces of this church remain, and the legend may be taken as an illustration of the rivalry that already existed between the people of Westminster and those of the City of London—a rivalry which has by no means completely died out today.

The story goes that Mellitus, Bishop of London, was to consecrate this new church on the site of some old Roman buildings on Thorney Island, but, the night before the ceremony, St. Peter appeared to a fisherman on the Thames and asked him to ferry him across. This the fisherman did, and, as a reward, St. Peter told him to cast his nets which drew in an enormous draught of salmon. When Mellitus arrived to consecrate the church, he was met by the fisherman who presented him with the salmon and informed him that the church had already been consecrated by St. Peter, supporting his statement by pointing out some candle wax on the floor—an indication that the service had been held.

That is the legend. The significance of it seems to lie in the consecration of the church by St. Peter, rather than a bishop of St. Paul. St. Paul for the City, St. Peter for Westminster seems to have been the point at issue, and the fact remains that Westminster Abbey is still the Collegiate Church of St. Peter.

Prints of the legend can be found in *The Life of St. Edward the Confessor* printed for the Roxburghe Club in 1920, and published by Oxford University Press, and the story is told in Matthew Arnold's poem, *Westminster Abbey*.

The name of Mellitus, who doesn't seem to have got much welcome either in the City or Westminster, can be seen in St. Paul's Cathedral, on the list of the Bishops of London, just by the entrance to the Galleries.

A scramasax: the dagger from which the Saxons got their name

Edward the Confessor's Palace and Abbey at Westminster

Whether the Westminster Abbey of the legend ever existed, there was certainly a small Benedictine Monastery on the site by about 750. This monastery was re-modelled by St. Dunstan about 960. Then, shortly after Edward the Confessor came to the throne, he set about rebuilding and enlarging it.

Close by, he built the Palace we've mentioned before as having such significance in the evolution of London as a capital city, which became the official London residence of Royalty until Henry VIII took over Whitehall Palace. Edward's Palace was enlarged by William the Conqueror and his son, William Rufus, who built Westminster Hall, destined to become the meeting-place of the Great Council, the forerunner of Parliament. The official title of the Houses of Parliament today remains the New Palace of Westminster.

Whether Edward built the palace in order to be near the City or near the monastery he was busy reconstructing is not clear. But his pious nature suggests that the refounding of the monastery was his principal interest.

Tradition has it that while in exile in Normandy during the Danish occupation he vowed to make a pilgrimage to Rome, to the shrine of St. Peter. His accession to the throne prevented him from carrying out his vow, and he was granted dispensation by the Pope on condition that he founded, or re-founded, a monastery to St. Peter.

The Confessor's church stood for two centuries, until it was rebuilt in the reign of Henry III, between 1220 and 1269. We can get some idea what it looked like from parts of the Bayeux Tapestry—Norman in design and vaster and more magnificent than any building Saxon England had seen before.

Foundations of the church have been discovered under the floor of the present nave; and reminders of Edward abound in the Abbey: the Chapel of the Confessor with its large shrine in the centre is itself the most sacred part of the abbey. Behind the altar, a 15th-century stone screen shows scenes from the life of Edward, including reliefs illustrating the Legend of the Ring.

This tells how Edward met a beggar who asked him for alms. The king had no money with him so he gave the beggar a ring. Not long afterwards, two pilgrims in the Holy Land met a stranger who revealed himself as St. John and handed them a ring—the ring which Edward, believing him to be a beggar, had given him. The pilgrims were told to return the ring to the Confessor and tell him that he would shortly join St. John in Paradise.

This story also appears on a 13th-century tile in the Chapter House of the Abbey.

Edward died on 5th January 1066, just eight days after the consecration of his new Abbey. Today the only surviving parts to be seen are just off the Cloisters: the Chamber of the Pyx, originally a sacristy, later the royal treasury and repository of the 'Pyx' (a chest containing the standards of reference for the minting of coins); and the Undercroft, now the home of the Abbey Museum.

The Legend of St. Mary Overy
(Southwark Cathedral)

The first church on the site of what is now Southwark Cathedral was founded in 616, by, if we accept the legend, Mary Overy.

Mary was the daughter of a ferryman, rich but miserly,

The buckle from the Sutton Hoo treasure (British Museum)

who spent little money on anything, but had a particular aversion to spending it on food. Consequently, his household lived very frugally—but not frugally enough for his satisfaction. In order to save even more money on the housekeeping, the ferryman struck on a brilliant idea—he would feign death. A household in mourning had to fast: a fast meant he wouldn't have to buy food.

So he pretended to die. Perhaps he also wanted to know how his family felt about him and how they would react on his death. If so he was in for something of a blow—the family were delighted. They raised whoopee! And not only that—they raised the 'corpse' as well. In the middle of the celebration, the furious ferryman suddenly sat up in his coffin. Unfortunately, this didn't quite have the effect he intended it to have. The celebration came to an abrupt halt, true; but the immediate effect was to so scare one of the servants out of her wits that she grabbed an oar and proceeded to batter the shrouded ferryman. This time the 'corpse' was really dead.

As a result of this, his daughter Mary inherited his wealth and was immediately in great demand as a wife. One suitor, although probably as much after her money as the others, was accepted by Mary, but then promptly got himself thrown off a horse and killed. All this was too much for Mary; she decided to get away from it all. Consequently, she used her fortune in the founding of a nunnery.

This is the legend, and certainly right up until the 16th century the church was dedicated to St. Mary Overy (or Overie)—the name most likely means 'over the river', either a nickname given to the ferryman or a name implying over the river from the City, in Southwark. The original nunnery was later absorbed by a college of priests in the 9th century, but the official name of Southwark Cathedral remains the Cathedral Church of St. Saviour and St. Mary Overy.

Other Places of Interest

St. Alphege's Church, Greenwich

In the year 1012, when English resistance was at its lowest ebb, the Danes seized Canterbury and carried off the primate, Bishop Alphege. He was brought to their camp at Greenwich ('wic' meant 'an occasional camp'). The Danes hoped for ransom, but Alphege refused to ask for it, and the cheated Danes battered him to death with ox-bones. St. Alphege's martyrdom is said to have taken place on the site of the present church in Greenwich. In the church there is a plaque to, and a stained glass window of, St. Alphege.

There is also a model of the Danes attacking London—their ship is moored at the mouth of the Fleet River and they are storming the walls of the City.

Barking Abbey

The Abbey at Barking, founded by Bishop Erkenwald in 666 and in which he installed his sister, Ethelburga, as Abbess, did not survive the Danish invasions. In 870, it lay in ruins, and not till a century later was any attempt made to rebuild it, when Edgar the Peaceful included it in his great revival of monasteries. No traces of this building now remain, the Abbey having been reconstructed in Norman times. Of this, which stood until the Dissolution of the Monasteries under Henry VIII, sections of a wall and the foundations can still be seen, close by St. Margaret's Church, itself originally founded in Norman times.

The Saxon Stone at Kingston-on-Thames

This stone, now displayed near the Guildhall in Kingston, is believed to have been used for the Coronations of seven kings of the late Saxon period, from 900 to 979, among them Edward the Elder, Athelstan (Alfred's son and grandson), Edgar the Peaceful, and Ethelred the Unready. Coins of the reigns of these kings can be seen in the plinth of the stone.

Anglo-Saxon and Viking Remains in Museums

Guildhall Museum

A map of Anglo-Saxon London showing pre-conquest church foundations:

St. Martin—Ludgate Hill
St. Gregory
St. Paul's
St. Augustine
St. Olave W. of wall of fort
St. Alphege—London Wall
St. Alban Wood Street
St. Mary Aldermary
St. Martin—Cannon Street
St. John, Walbrook
St. Swithin—Cannon Street
St. Pancras, off King Street
St. Ethelburga
St. Botolph—Bishopsgate

St. Botolph—Aldgate
St. Botolph off Lower Thames St.
All Hallows Berkynge
St. Olave—Hart St.
St. Olave—Southwark
St. Mildred, W. of Princes Street
St. Benet Fink—Threadneedle Street
St. Edmund—Lombard Street
All Hallows—Lombard Street

Site of Folk mote—North side of St. Paul's
Site of King Ethelbert's Palace—Wood Street, north of St. Albans

Photographs of the shaft of an Anglo-Saxon Cross
Photographs of the wooden foundations of an Anglo-Saxon hall, part of the farm found on the site of the Treasury, Downing St.
Amber beads
Chatelaine for carrying housekeeping keys 9th–10th century (a simple chain rather like a modern bath-plug chain)
Part (side) of a drinking horn

Range of spear heads (6th–10th C.)

Hoard of jewellery found in Cheapside, of pewter—rings, brooches, beads, and ear rings—probably belonged to a jeweller as some of items are unfinished

Small cooking pot, late Saxon, found in Lombard St.

Loom weights

Bone comb—Cheapside

The end of a drinking horn found in Fetter Lane (Viking)

A 12th-century bronze hanging lamp

British Museum: Manuscript Room
Illuminated Manuscripts

New Minster (Winchester) Charter—granted by King Edgar in 966

Beowulf: late 9th century

A whole case of manuscripts in Latin and Anglo-Saxon

Bede's *Ecclesiastical History of the English Nation*: late 8th century

Bede's *Life of St. Cuthbert* in Latin. Late 12th century

Bibles (Case II)

Bosworth Psalter—late 10th-century Latin with Anglo-Saxon between the lines in small print

Lindisfarne Gospels 698

(Magna Carta Room, off Manuscript Room)

Open at the 'Carpet' page (overall design) and the beginning of St. Mark's Gospel

Anglo-Saxon Chronicle

11th-century manuscript

London Museum

Anglo-Saxon and Danish swords—from the 6th, 8th, 9th, 10th, and/or 11th centuries

Shield Boss (round)

6th-century bronze bowl

Viking horse equipment: spur, cheek piece

Strips of gold-plated copper with incised ornaments in Anglo-Scandinavian style of interlaced patterns. Strips for nailing on wood. Use uncertain

A large bell, uncommon in the south of England; used in early church in Wales, Scotland, and Ireland. Found at Mortlake

Ring of plated gold wire (Moorgate, 9th–11th century)

Viking bracelet from Westminster with incised decoration

Viking bone combs

Bone chess pieces with pegs for inserting in holes in the board. A game introduced from the Orient during the 10th century

Bone counters for backgammon or a similar game (2 inches in diameter). Date uncertain

Bone toggle

Late Saxon comb with case

10th century bone spoons and knife handles

Ox ribs, carved with designs which may be an artist's doodling or roughs for a proper carving

Grater

Weaving comb

London Bridge Hoard from a Viking ship which was involved in the battle near the Bridge

> Battle axes
> Spear heads
> Grappling iron
> Smith's tongs
> Saxon axes and knives and pots

From an Anglo-Saxon cemetery at Mitcham—by Mitcham station—sword, shield boss, brooches, bowls

Cuming Museum, Southwark

A grappling iron from near London Bridge

Norman England

The Normans, formerly Vikings from Scandinavia who had established themselves in France as a powerful Duchy, quickly and firmly established themselves in England as the ruling aristocracy. Their number was small, but such was the existing state of English society that the replacement of the Saxon nobility by Norman barons in all positions of importance in Church and State gave them effective rule over the entire country. This numerical inferiority meant too, that, in the long run, the Norman was absorbed into the English race and distinctions between the two races disappeared.

But the immediate effect of the Conquest was the Norman subjugation of the Saxons, mainly by military force. Castles, unseen in England till this time, began to dot the landscape, both for protection against attack by invaders and, more importantly, as warnings of Norman military power against possible insurrection within the country. The first years of William's reign were spent in the

'Harrying of the North', quelling rebellion in Yorkshire and Durham. Less troublesome for him, but more memorable to us, was the activity of Hereward the Wake around Ely.

William rewarded his followers by granting them lands. These were held by barons on condition of service to the king, mainly military: each 'tenant-in-chief', as the land-owning barons were called, had to provide the king with a number of armed knights. To do so, many tenants-in-chief offered parts of their land on similar terms to their own followers, thus creating military sub-tenancies. (The land granted to any person was called that person's 'fief' or 'feud': hence the word feudal applied to this system of land-holding.)

The advantages of the system to the king were obvious: all land in England was his, held by him as feudal lord; a readily assembled army was always available. But there were disadvantages too, mainly in the danger of an individual baron becoming too powerful and using his military sub-tenants for his own purposes. William saw this, and not only did he ensure that the estates of each baron were well scattered throughout the country, thus avoiding too much accumulation of power in one area, he also, in 1086, demanded that all sub-tenants should take an oath of fealty direct to himself. The sub-tenant was to be 'his man' rather than a tool of the barons.

The effect of this system was to lower the stock of the peasant even further, to place him firmly at the bottom of the 'feudal pyramid'. The tenant-in-chief became lord of the manor, and anyone living in his manor virtually his property. The 'freeman' no longer existed, and it is unlikely that it would have brightened his lot any to know that his further fall in status was necessary to the creation of a more strongly ordered society.

Order in fact was the key-note to the age. Not only military order and discipline, but order in the more civil-

A penny of Harold who was defeated at the Battle of Hastings

ised sense as well. Men were at last throwing off a barbaric state of mind and a genuine feeling for a civilised way of life was taking over. The goal of Alfred and the past mentors of the Church was being achieved, and it may appear ironic that the call for order was now being directed against the Church itself. The demand for Church reform was two-fold: a general one throughout Europe brought on by a near-collapse of Church organisation and a decline in the standard of behaviour of churchmen; and, in England, by a more personal struggle between King and Papacy as to which of them should have control of the English Church.

William was a devout Christian, but he was also King, and to put his country under the overlordship of the Pope, as Gregory VII demanded, was something William refused to do. The Christian fervour of William and his fellow Normans can be seen in the vast number of churches they built; his opposition to papal rule in the firm control he kept over the organisation of the English Church itself, a control continued and, unlike William's, exploited by his sons, William II and Henry I.

William was in many ways a cruel and tyrannical man, given to fits of violence, but when he behaved ruthlessly it was usually for political reasons. He was, above all, a politician, shrewd and clever. He had maintained he was a legitimate claimant to the throne and had wished to establish a more balanced Anglo-Norman kingdom, but the iron glove was forced on him and he had the hand to wear it. Nonetheless, he made no more break with the past than seemed necessary and preserved most of the Saxon institutions he found—mainly because they served his own purpose in strengthening the power of the monarchy.

Norman knights from the Bayeux Tapestry. This shows the pointed helmets, conical shields, and long mail coats.

It was to explore his power, to discover the resources of his kingdom and how they might best be used, that William ordered the compilation of the Domesday Book. He wanted to know who ran what, and whether they ought to; he also wanted to know who he could collect tax from, and whether it could be increased.

William, and his successors, were constantly seeking money. They needed it not only for government and military purposes, but to continue their great programme of church-building. It was for this reason that they fostered the Jews and encouraged their settlement, which had begun with the arrival of Jewish traders in the wake of the Conquest. The Norman king saw how they could be used for his own ends. He became sole protector of the Jews—a protection needed since the Jews were hated both as money-lenders and, in that great Christian age, as enemies of Christ. The Jews became the king's serfs, but they gained protection—in return for which the king called for money from them whenever he required it.

William, unpopular as he and many of his measures may have been, gave England its strongest government since Canute. His son, William Rufus, reigned for thirteen years, continuing the strong rule with even greater unpopularity. He was killed, rather mysteriously, by an arrow while hunting in the New Forest (one of the most hated Norman innovations was the creation of vast forest areas set aside for royal stag-hunting), and was succeeded by his brother, Henry I.

Henry proved to be a much better ruler than Rufus, having inherited more of the Conqueror's political shrewdness and ability. To begin with, he issued a Charter of Liberties, confirming the ancient laws of the people—a sensible conciliatory move after the abuses perpetrated by William Rufus. At the same time Henry turned his attention to strengthening the machinery of royal administration, both in local affairs, where royal justices were established to sit in on shire courts, and in the king's court itself. The Conqueror had continued the meetings between himself and the great men of the country. These great Councils were held three times a year, at Christmas, Easter, and Whitsun, presided over by the king, wearing his crown for the occasion.

But the routine day-to-day business of government was accumulating, and to meet this, a smaller council of barons was created. Then the need for specialisation was seen, first of all in finance. The Exchequer (from which comes today's Chancellor of the Exchequer) was devised. The name comes from the chequered effect of the cloth used for counting out the money received. The cloth was marked out with horizontal lines, crossed by six vertical lines, creating columns for pence, shillings, pounds, tens of pounds, hundreds, thousands, and tens of thousands.

The Norman kings of England also had their lands in France to run—no easy task: Henry I, in fact, had to reoccupy Normandy. To strengthen his hold on French affairs he made an alliance with the house of Anjou, an unpopular move with many Normans who hated the Angevins. On Henry's death, his chosen successor was his daughter Matilda, but as she was betrothed to the Count of Anjou's son, there was great opposition to her. A rival candidate was Stephen of Boulogne, Matilda's cousin.

It was now that the citizens of London came into their own as a powerful independent voice—they claimed their right to say in the election of the king; and elected Stephen. The country was split, and for twenty years of civil war remained split by rival supporters of Stephen and Matilda. In 1154, the years of anarchy were brought to an end when Matilda's son, Henry, succeeded to the throne—the first of the Plantagenets who were to rule England for some 250 years. (The name, Plantagenet, probably derives from the father of Henry's habit of wearing a sprig of broom—genesta or genet—in his cap.)

Henry II (1154–89) was an active, many-sided man who quickly re-established a firm control on the country and gave it thirty years of security and prosperity. He brought the barons, who had taken advantage of the years of anarchy to build up personal power, back under

The Tower of London: a view of the south side of the keep (White Tower) showing the original Norman windows.

St. Andrew's Church, Greensted, Ongar; above is a detail of the wooden Saxon walls made from split tree trunks. In the lower photograph on the left is a view of the interior of the church which has the oldest surviving wooden walls in the country.

St. Mary's, East Ham: a fine example of Norman church architecture. The photograph above shows the blind arcading and the anchorite's window for watching the service.

St. Bartholomew the Great: a view of the Norman arcading round the sanctuary.

Vikings attacking London: the model from St. Alphage's Church, Greenwich.

The legend of St. Peter at Westminster: the fisherman presents a salmon to Bishop Mellitus. (Photographs by Michael Taylor)

royal control and demolished their private unlicensed castles. He further strengthened and expanded the system of royal administration, especially in matters of the Law. The justices established in Henry I's reign were now sent on a more regular circuit of the shire courts, and it was through them that Henry introduced the germs of the Trial by Jury system with which we are familiar today. The germs, no more: the twelve good men and true were no more than men of the neighbourhood whose local knowledge was called upon to help the royal justice reach the correct settlement of a dispute. It is from Henry's reign that we may trace the development of our modern central courts.

Henry II, the great law-giver, despite the fact that most of his legal innovations were made with a view to increasing royal power, was popular with the people. 'All men loved him, for he did good justice and made peace.' Yet perhaps not all men; men of the Church saw him in a different light. Henry's aim was to strengthen and increase the power of the crown; to achieve this he had to confirm and extend his control over the Church, which, under the weak and troubled rule of Stephen, had added to its power.

Henry appointed his Chancellor, Thomas Becket, as Archbishop of Canterbury. But his former friend, who had assisted him in his legal reforms, refused to back his reforms of the Church, insisting on the Church's right to deal with its own criminals—a right which Henry claimed for the king's courts. The story of this quarrel, resulting in the murder of Becket in Canterbury Cathedral, is too well known to require elaboration here, even had there been space to do so. The final outcome was that Henry won many of the rights he claimed from the Church and succeeded in increasing his control over it.

Henry II's extension of royal power, and his advanced administration and tight system of government proved strong enough to sustain the non-rule of his successor,

Richard I. Better known as the Lion Heart, Richard spent only six months of his reign (1189–1199) in England. His kingdom to him was little more than a source of revenue for his Crusades in the Holy Land against the Mohammedans. Most of this money came from a continuation of the practice whereby the towns (which had been growing since the Conquest) used the profits from trade to buy privileges for themselves. Many new towns sprang up and existing towns developed; but the most important, and by now the capital city, was London.

Another scene from the Bayeux Tapestry which shows servants preparing a meal. The two on the left are turning a spit, and the man on the right is putting food on a dish.

Norman London

William, King, greets William, Bishop, and Gosfrith, Portreeve, and all the burgesses within London, French and English, friendly. And I give you to know that I will that ye be to all those laws worthy that ye were in King Edward's day. And I will that every child be his father's heir after his father's day and I will not suffer that any man offer you any wrong. God keep you.

So runs the Charter (now in the Guildhall) issued by William the Conqueror to the city of London as an assurance that he would respect their privileges. The all-conquering William was forced to act warily with regard to London, already to a certain extent self-governing, conscious of its supremacy over other cities, proud and tenacious of its traditions and privileges, and ready to defend them with 'a formidable and large body of men'. William was right to be wary. Immediately after his coronation he moved to Barking, outside the city but still near enough to pounce should trouble arise. To prevent it from doing so, he balanced his conciliatory measure with a threatening one. He had built 'certain strongholds in the town against the fickleness of the vast and fierce populace'. Two of these castles were on the west side of

67

the town: Baynard's Castle, of which (having been destroyed in the Great Fire) the only trace now remaining is the name, Castle Baynard, of the small wharf off Upper Thames Street; and the Tower of Montfichet, which stood near Ludgate Circus, and which was later the site of a Blackfriars Monastery, destroyed in the Dissolution.

But it was the castle in the east of the city that most impressed the Londoners—the White Tower of what was later to become the Tower of London. This was begun in 1078, and whatever its effect, William was still, eight years later, wary of offending the Londoner—or so it appears from the fact that the Domesday Book, that great survey of the resources of the country, did not include London in its investigation.

Then, under Henry I, they received another Charter of Liberties, mainly reaffirming existing rights in commerce and self-government, but also allowing certain new privileges, among them exemption from the new process of Trial by Battle, but more importantly the right to appoint their own sheriff and assess their own taxes. Another king had been compelled to talk terms with the Londoners; before long, as we have seen, they were to claim the right to elect the king himself (Stephen).

But it was in the reign of Henry II that London really came into its own. The growth of bureaucracy, the creation of more and more royal servants, specialists in financial and legal administration, necessitated permanent quarters—these were established in London: first, Westminster became the seat of permanent justices; later (in fact, after Henry's death) the Exchequer was moved from Winchester to London.

The king no longer had to move about the country as in Saxon times, but he did, as an Angevin, have to move between this country and his territories in France. London, by its geographical position, was an ideal centre for the king. Trading centre, now centre of finance and administration, London at last became capital city.

Life in Norman London

...There are many folk in the city, and they are housed close together and are more crowded early and late than other people are ... When the citizens are thus crowded together, whether at their drinking or elsewhere, they might kill each other, and the city would never enjoy steady tranquillity.

London begins to be more familiar to us. That, in fact, is an extract from the Norman Londoners' argument against their having to submit to inquests under oath—the essence being that 'great mischief might arise' to anyone who swore in court against his neighbour because of the social conditions. Yet another example of their claim to special privileges, but more interesting to us now for the glimpse it gives us of the city at that time—congested and prone to violence.

It's likely that the Londoners rather exaggerated the case so as to win their argument, but certainly, compared with other towns, crowding, if not over-crowding, was already appearing as a hazard of London life. By 1200, more than 20,000 people were living there; it had one of the largest populations in Europe. Trade, of course, was the main reason for living in the city; not only trade with abroad, but the local transactions between town and country.

London as a Country Town

Norman London, despite its size and its cosmopolitan outlook, was in many respects still a country town. The citizens had grazing rights in the surrounding countryside—in Epping Forest, for example; and they also had hunting rights (confirmed in Henry I's Charter) in Middlesex, Hertfordshire, the Chilterns, and in Kent as far as the River Cray. Ploughmen and herds lived in the town as well as traders and craftsmen. From William Fitzstephen's graphic if somewhat over-enthusiastic and uncritical picture of his beloved London of the time, we hear that 'On the north Side are Fields for Pasture, and open Meadows, very pleasant; among which the River Waters do flow, and the Wheels of the Mills are turned about with a delightful Noise'.

But if the Pastures are 'pleasant', they're nothing in comparison with 'the arable Lands [which] are no hungry Pieces of Gravel Ground, but like the rich Fields of Asia, which bring plentiful Corn, and fill the Barns of those that till them with a dainty Crop of the Fruits of Ceres'.

Within the town itself there were gardens and orchards, and, linking town and country, an agricultural market just outside the walls, at Smithfield, still a market today. Smithfield is derived from Smoothfield—but let Fitzstephen describe it: 'Without one of the Gates is a certain Field, plain [smooth] both in Name and Situation. Every Friday, except some greater Festival come in the Way [such as a tournament or a fair: see the separate sections on both of these] there is a brave Sight of gallant Horses to be sold: Many came out of the City to buy or look on, to wit, Earls, Barons, Knights, Citizens, all resorting thither. It is a pleasant Sight there to behold the Nags, well fleshed, sleek and shining. . . .'

And not just Nags, there were also 'Swine with long Flanks, Cows with full Udders, Oxen of immense Size and woolly Sheep'.

The picture we should have of London, then, is of town and country life mingling in the streets, of merchants going about their business while herdsmen drive their stock to and from market and grazing-land, on occasion over London Bridge, as we shall see in a moment.

London as a Trading Centre

Agricultural though London was then, it was soon to sever any close connection with the countryside. As a centre of trade and commerce it remains today one of the busiest and most important in the world. Then as now, Smithfield was a market; then as now, Billingsgate was a busy fish market, and on the wharves between there and Queenshithe traders from many countries could be seen and heard. (The name 'Queenshithe' may have derived either from its coming into the possession of Henry I's wife, or from the mill for grinding corn landed there, which was called a 'quern'.)

Merchants in London were used to trading with Scandinavian countries, with various parts of France, and with Italy and further afield. The new connections with Normandy and Anjou increased trade with these areas. The new peace and security within England itself led to greater yield from the land: there was sufficient corn for some to be exported; most important of all, safer grazing led to bigger flocks of sheep, and wool became our principal export. Imports included Flanders cloth, Scandinavian fur, spices from the Orient, wine from Bordeaux, and yet more wine from Bordeaux.

71

The Norman English were great wine drinkers; it's been estimated that consumption per head was three times what it is today. England was one of the chief importers of wine in Europe (by the middle of the 15th century it amounted to one-third of all the country's imports). One of the main stimuli to the wine trade came with Henry II's marriage to Eleanor of Aquitaine which brought under his rule the whole of the west of France: Normandy, Anjou, Poitou, Aquitaine, and Gascony—all vineyard areas. The principal vintner's wharf was Dowgate, at the mouth of the Walbrook.

Imports were, of course, subject to duty; these taxes were collected at the Tower. Ships on the river had also to pay tolls mostly out of their cargo. In the case of a wine ship, for example, the toll was two flagons of the wine on board. This too was payable to the Constable of the Tower, a gentleman in whose way came many things which to modern cynical minds appear more in the nature of 'perks' than anything else: for example, all the swans below London Bridge were his, and also, more spectacularly, any cattle that fell off the Bridge. Commercial centre or not, there's no getting away from the agricultural side of London life.

The London merchants had first claim (after the king,

*A coin showing
the head of
William the
Conqueror*

of course) on any goods brought into the city; only if they didn't want them were the goods then offered to the rest of the country. It is about this time that we first see the merchants forming themselves into 'gilds'. These will be dealt with in greater detail in the third book of this series, for not until the Middle Ages did these guilds attain their full power. Suffice it to say here that these early guilds were formed to protect the interests of the small trader, to ensure fairness both in the sharing of trade and in pricing, and to prevent outsiders (merchants or tradesmen from other towns) from setting up in business within their town.

One of the first guilds we know of was the Weavers'; their charter, granted them by Henry II, confirmed their privileges and forbade the practice of weaving in London and Southwark to anyone outside their guild. The Bakers' guild was also established about this time. But it must be stressed that these early guilds had none of the power which the later guilds assumed.

The Contrasts of Norman London

In this Place, the Calmness of the Air doth mollify Men's Minds, not corrupting them with Lusts, but preserving them from savage and rude Behaviour, and seasoning their Inclinations with a more kind and free Temper.

The description is again, unmistakably, by William Fitzstephen, and must therefore be taken with a grain of salt. We must balance his picture with that already glimpsed of a potentially violent, possibly congested area. The 'fierce populace' of William the Conqueror's time may doubtless have become tamer by Fitzstephen's (1170) but it's unlikely the Air had calmed them that much. Violence was sure to break out in the narrow, dingy streets of the poorer quarters; and in higher circles there was the organised violence of the tournament (see the section on Tournaments).

Fitzstephen stresses the beauty of the house-and-garden suburbs; he has little to say of the hovels in the slums. And while it is true that the nobility and the Church (followed later by the wealthier tradesmen) had houses above the standard of the rest of the country, it is equally true that the majority of the dwellings were no more than just habitable. The houses owned by the Church were generally the finest, and they remained so in London throughout the Middle Ages.

Sports and Pastimes

The citizens of Norman London were a lively, energetic people, and this is seen as much in their sports and pastimes as in their business activity. Fitzstephen describes their sports and pastimes as 'very plentiful' and here there is no need to quibble with him.

The Tournaments and Fairs held at Smithfield will be described elsewhere. These were by and large spectator events; the true vigour of the Norman Londoner, particularly the young, can be seen in their mock-fights, their bull-baiting, and bear-baiting. Fitzstephen describes their Summer Sports as 'Leaping, Shooting, Wrestling, casting of Stones, and throwing of Javelins fitted with Loops for the Purpose, which they strive to fling beyond the Mark; they also use Bucklers, like fighting Men. As for the Maidens, they have their Exercise of Dancing and Tripping until Moon-light'.

Strenuous activities requiring youth and agility. What of the older and less agile? Well, there were many ale-houses in the town; but apart from that there were chess and draughts, both extremely popular at this time. If chess, a game demanding skill, patience, and peaceful concentration, seems to go against the active tenor of the time, it may be that, as one chronicler puts it, chess was the hobby of the wise; draughts the hobby of knights.

But most pastimes had something of a military flavour.

Fitzstephen describes one of the mock fights; this one not between opponents but between man and pole, the pole being set in the middle of the Thames. It was in fact a kind of water-jousting. The pole had a target on it, and the youth tried to hit the target with a spear from a boat which was rowed past it. If he succeeded in hitting it hard enough to break the spear, while himself remaining upright, he'd won the game; if on the other hand his spear didn't break, it didn't matter if he'd remained upright or not because he was promptly tossed into the river by the oarsmen, who rowed on and left him. Fitzstephen doesn't mention swimming as a favourite pastime; one can only hope it was. Or perhaps if the loser floated as far as the Tower, the Constable claimed him.

This fight on the river took place during the Easter holidays. In winter the great sport was ice-skating, or more accurately for the majority, ice-sliding. The nearest thing to skates they had were animal bones which they strapped to their shoes; but these appear to have been used more like skis than skates since they did 'hold Stakes in their Hands, headed with Sharp Iron, which sometimes they strike against the Ice'. There was a very Norman sort of snow-balling: 'snowballs' were 'Heaps of Ice, as if it were great Mill-stones'.

Children's games too reflect the military tendency of the age; their games were mini-versions of the grownups. Their toys, if again military, were little different from the toys of today, although of course less sophisticated. Dolls for the girls; toy soldiers for the boys was the general rule. And there were wooden models, tops, and toy horses too. Boys in pairs often staged fights between two wooden soldiers, which were jointed to give moveable arms and legs, the feet being weighted to keep the figures balanced as the boys walked them about by means of a cord through their middles, each boy holding one end of each of the two cords.

Outside the city, the Londoners could use their cours-

Three Norman chessmen which are now in the British Museum

ing rights to hunt fox or deer in their allotted areas; but anyone entering a royal forest to hunt did so at peril of death: killing a hare was punished by mutilation, killing a deer, by hanging. (These royal forests, reserved for the king to hunt in, covered about a third of the country, and, needless to say, were a source of grievance to the people.)

By the end of the 12th century, Londoners were already showing a taste for great ceremonial occasions, processions, and banquets. In this they were probably influenced by William Rufus who gave lavish banquets to his followers, and in fact, probably built his magnificent Westminster Hall in order to give even bigger and better banquets. When Richard the Lion Heart returned after his captivity, the Londoners gave him a welcome of great pomp and ceremony—in return for which, Richard promptly imposed new taxes. This, however, did not succeed in dampening the citizens' growing enthusiasm for ceremony.

The Changing Face of Norman London

The Norman way of life was so different in many respects from our own that it's hard for us to get a real feeling of what it was like to live at that time. But in one respect perhaps we can come very near: the Londoners in Norman times must have been as used to having new buildings appear seemingly almost overnight as Londoners today. And if our new sky-scrapers and multi-storey blocks of flats are higher than anything in London at the turn of the 20th century, the same applied to the buildings growing up at the turn of the 12th. Only Edward the Confessor's Church could have prepared the Londoners for what was to come, being already Norman in plan. But even Edward's buildings were to grow even bigger (his Palace acquiring the new Westminster Hall, thanks to William Rufus) and the three new castles were something they were totally unprepared for. And all over the place the new churches were popping up.

Few of these have survived till today (for those which have, see the section on Norman Buildings), even the bigger Abbeys and Cathedrals which must have been so important in their time. Many of these are commemorated in street names. For example, in Bermondsey there is an Abbey Street and a Cluny Place, which remind us that there was once a Bermondsey Abbey, a Cluniac foundation affiliated to the parent Abbey at Cluny in Burgundy. Founded by Alwin Child (the father of the first Mayor of London) in 1082, it stood on the site of the present parish church, St. Mary Magdalen. All that remains from the Abbey are some decorated capitals, but its importance at the time can be judged from the fact that Henry II held a 'Parliament' there in 1154.

So, big new buildings now, big new buildings then. But if we in the second half of the 20th century are about to lose a London Bridge, the Londoners in the second half of the 12th were about to gain one.

Edward the Confessor's Abbey from the Bayeux Tapestry

The old Saxon wooden bridge, built in the reign of Edgar, was burned down in 1135. The building of the new bridge was ordered by Henry II, but the idea of building it in stone came from the chaplain of St. Mary Colechurch in Cheapside. This chaplain, Peter de Colechurch, was put in charge of the building, which proved very difficult because of the strength of the tidal flow and river currents. Construction, begun in 1176, was not completed until 1210. Money towards the building of the bridge was contributed by the people of London, by everyone from nobles down.

It was 900 feet long, 30 feet wide, and had 19 narrow arches. There were gatehouses at either side, and in the middle stood a chapel dedicated to St. Thomas of Canterbury. (On Peter de Colechurch's death he was buried in the crypt of this chapel.) But the most immediately striking feature of the bridge if you look at a pictorial reproduction of it—one of the best is a painting by Canaletto—is that there were houses and shops all the way across it.

These were probably not part of the original plans for the bridge, only coming to be built later. Whether they should have been built is questionable; certainly the bridge tended to collapse from time to time. In 1437, for example, two arches and the Gatehouse on the Southwark side gave way. Incidents like these no doubt ensured the continuing popularity of 'London Bridge Is Falling Down'. Nevertheless, it stood successfully for more than six hundred years, being finally pulled down in 1832, following the completion in the previous year of the present bridge—which, in its turn, is about to vanish from the face of London.

There is little doubt that the Londoners of the time were enthusiastic about their new bridge—at a later date people even used to leave legacies to it—and perhaps, with the long time it took to be built, we should have included Watching-the-Workmen-on-the-Bridge amongst the Norman Londoners' pastimes.

Today the only trace of the old bridge (though from a much later period) is one of the 'shelters' for pedestrians which now stands in the forecourt of Guy's Hospital. The forecourt of St. Magnus the Martyre and the steps beside Southwark Cathedral mark the old entries to the bridge on the north and south side respectively.

Norman Armour

The Normans were masters of the art of war and they advanced the techniques of fighting in many ways, notably in offensive and defensive strategy—the feigned flight tempting the enemy to break his line, followed by the swift charge of mounted knights through the gaps. This tactic ultimately won the Battle of Hastings for them. Their use of archers also introduced the technique of fighting at long-range.

They made improvements too in their weapons and

79

armour. Their armour gave much greater over-all protection. The coat of mail, the 'hauberk', was much longer than the Saxon's 'byrnie', and continued over the head, balaclava-fashion. The Norman knight wore a conical iron helmet, close-fitting and with a 'nasal' or nose-guard. His hauberk was slit at the bottom to allow greater ease of movement when mounted; his shield, made of metal, and shaped rather like a kite, had likewise been devised for horse-back fighting, the added length offering protection to the thigh. He wore thick stockings made of cloth, called 'chausses', which were cross-gartered with leather thongs. The knight's hauberk was leather, covered with metal rings or plates.

The model of a Norman knight from the Wallace Collection. This shows the nose guard which was a feature of the helmet.

The armour of the infantryman was similar, if simpler, lacking the extra refinements required by the cavalryman. His hauberk was often made of thick linen, quilted or padded, and covered with leather bands studded with metal. The bowman, however, required little or no armour for his long-range role in the fighting: a thick cloth tunic fastened with a belt of the same material, dividing below the waist into wide knee-length trousers.

Later, with the great prosperity in the reign of Henry II and the increased skill of craftsmanship, the armour of the wealthy knight began to take on a more glamorous appearance: chain-mail became finer, swords and shields more magnificent, and participation in the jousting tournaments created the first team colours, as it were— the banners and devices and the silk coats worn over the armour by which the participants could be recognised by their supporters.

Norman Dress

Out of armour, the Norman noble wore a long tunic of linen or wool, sleeveless and open at the sides, over a sleeved linen under-tunic. On top of this he might wear a cloak, fastened at the shoulder by a knot and a ring brooch. His legs were covered by 'chausses', and he wore leather shoes.

The Norman lady wore a full-length tunic, the 'bliaut', wide-flowing from the hip. Again, an under-tunic supplied the wrist-length sleeves, and it was also revealed at the neck by the low-cut outer garment, which was laced down the sides. Her semi-circular cloak was tied at the front by a cord. Her jewelled belt, which encircled the body twice, was likewise tied at the front by means of knotting.

The dress of the lower classes changed little throughout the years, remaining the simple smock-style tunic. But again, prosperity and the new imports brought in

Norman costume: the man wears a long tunic and cloak while the woman has a full-length 'bliaut'

with the increase of trade led to new luxury in the clothes of the rich. Robes of Flanders cloth and furs from Scandinavia provided feelings of both luxury and warmth—the latter being of possibly greater importance, as we are about to see.

The Normans, incidentally, were generally clean-shaven and, unlike the Saxons and Danes, wore their hair short. Women wore their hair in long plaits and covered their heads with a kind of veil, held by a circle of metal.

Dwellings

The castles and baronial halls where the nobility lived were large, and, as might be expected, (especially with open, unglazed windows) extremely draughty—hence the need for fur and other warm materials in their clothing. It was generally colder inside a hall than it was out of doors, but, fortunately, the Normans, both upper and lower classes, spent most of their time in the open air.

These halls, however, were great improvements on the halls of the Saxon nobility; for one thing, they were built of stone (building will be discussed in greater detail elsewhere). Rooms continued to be large, and privacy again was difficult—at least in the day-time. For night-time there were now some smaller rooms for use as bed-chambers. But the halls and castles remained to begin with places built in the interest of defence rather than of home comfort. The great hall of the castle, for example, was usually on the second floor, both for security reasons and for reasons of lighting—higher up, windows could be made bigger since there was less danger from attack. The needs of defence dictated nearly everything in the planning of these buildings.

But, as the country became more secure and as the nobles started building manor-houses, more consideration was given to comfort. The Englishman's castle was becoming his home.

More and better furniture was introduced. If seating and dining requirements remained simple—trestle-tables, wooden benches, and stools—sleeping requirements were catered for more carefully. The Norman bed was large and richly ornamented. And decoration for its own sake began to appear in incidental objects like chests and coffers which were elaborately decorated.

The houses of the people were, naturally, smaller, but in the later period not dissimilar in conception to the manor-house. There was a hall on the ground floor, with a private room, or 'solar', above. In the back, perhaps no more than a lean-to, was the kitchen. By the 12th century, there was at least some house-building in stone—if no more, in many places, than in the stone wall between the houses, the 'party-wall' as it was called. A Building Regulation of Richard I's time calls for an increase in building with stone in the city of London—a sensible recommendation in the light of congested living (the 'party-wall' in itself shows how closely crammed together the houses already were) and the frequent danger of fires. In 1077 and again in 1087 London had been swept by fire, the latter destroying St. Paul's Cathedral.

The houses then, generally built of wood and with thatched roofs, offered no defence against the fires; rather the opposite, encouraging their spread. Fire regulations there were: ladders had to be kept in houses with more than one floor; buckets and barrels of water had to be kept at the front door; hooks, chains, and ropes had to be readily available for pulling down burning houses— but these were clearly insufficient to prevent a fire spreading over the entire concentrated area of the city (some idea of its concentration may be got from the number of parish churches existing at the time—126 in all). The need to build in stone, then, was obvious, but it took many years for the wooden houses to disappear completely.

A whalebone carving of the Madonna and Child which is in the British Museum

Food

Food, in variety, cooking, and consumption, changed little from Saxon to Norman times. Perhaps imports from the Orient had added some spice to the meals of the wealthy, but in general the menu remained the same—fish, beef, mutton, pork, and poultry; the quality depending on the price you could afford to pay. Fish, of course, was the Friday food, and the only thing permitted for eating during Lent. Eggs were forbidden during this period, and so we get the tradition of the Easter Egg—hard-boiled in coloured water, blessed by the priest on Good Friday, then eaten as part of the celebrations on Easter Sunday.

Bread, as we know it today, was non-existent. It was generally baked on the ashes of the fire and made from rye with no yeast added. The slice of bread was frequently used as a plate for the rest of the food and only eaten when that was finished.

Cooking at home still depended on being affluent enough to afford an oven. The nobility, of course, were well endowed both with cooking facilities and the servants to make use of them. In the Bayeux Tapestry we can see the food being boiled and roasted and served at table on the spits used for the roasting.

The townspeople, however, especially the citizens of London, still depended on the 'take-away' cookshop, many more of which had sprung up. And offering greater facilities as well—William Fitzstephen lavishes great praise on them, especially one in Vintry Ward, near the river, which provided service 'at whatever Hours of Night or Day'. A 24-hour service, then, offering 'any Dish of Meat, roast, fried, or boiled; Fish both small and great; ordinary Flesh for the poorer sort, and more dainty for the Rich, as Venison and Fowl'—all available ready-made to eat there or take away.

Cookshops, and ale-shops too. Fitzstephen's only criticism of London ('A good City, when it hath a good Lord') are the two plagues of Fires and 'immoderate Drinking of idle Fellows'.

Fairs

Ordinary foods and agricultural produce were bought and sold at the weekly market. But every so often the Fair would come to town, a much more elaborate kind of market where luxury goods, unattainable locally, were on sale. By the end of the 12th century, these fairs, only rarely heard of previously, had become regular events. Trade and business was the main object, but the locals seized on the three or four days during which it was held to turn it into a great occasion—a welcome break in the routine of their existence. It became as much an entertainment as a business affair—the Fair, as it remains today, shows how much the entertainment factor took over from the commercial, to the extent of eliminating it altogether.

Fairs had to be licensed, and, to begin with, they were restricted to certain appointed locations. They were often given the names of the patron saints of the areas in which they were located, and held on appropriate dates associated with these saints; St. Ives, St. Giles—in London, St. Bartholomew.

Bartholomew's Fair

In 1133, Rahere, the founder of St. Bartholomew's Priory, was granted a Charter by Henry I, allowing him to hold a fair in the market beside the priory—Smithfield. Bartholomew's Fair, then, was one of the greater Festivals mentioned by Fitzstephen as coming in the way of the regular horse-market.

The Fair rapidly grew in popularity and became in time *the* great London fair (it lasted until 1855, but was probably at its peak in the early 1600s). Rahere used the

The Seal of William the Conqueror

profits from the fair to endow his Priory and Hospital, a fact which the throngs of Londoners probably scarcely knew, or little cared about if they did. They were there to enjoy themselves. Commerce took a back seat; entertainment was the thing—bear-baiting, dancing and singing, juggling, and exhibitions of freaks and monsters. Street singers, the ballad mongers, were greatly appreciated, and in turn greatly appreciated the money collected from the crowds.

Astute inn-keepers moved out of their normal pubs and set up booths at the fair. For example, a Mr. Thomas Dale of the Crown Tavern in Aldgate opened the Turk's Head Musick Booth at Smithfield, providing not only liquor but entertainment: 'Here is a glass of good Wine, Mum, Syder, Beer, Ale and all other sorts of Liquors to be sold; and where you will likewise be entertained with good Musick, Singing and Dancing.' Acrobatic dancing at that—the dancers included a young woman who juggled with fourteen wine glasses, turning all the time 'above a Hundred Times as fast as a Windmill'.

Tournaments

Another of the great Festivals mentioned by Fitzstephen as taking place in Smithfield was probably the Tournament.

To begin with the Tournament was little better than a free fight, without the fixed rules attached to them in later years. They probably arose out of boredom rather than anything else; the Norman was essentially a man of action, and, in times of peace, the knight, cheated of his professional activities and surrounded by servants who did everything for him, had little to sustain him. The excitement of the joust, then, was something to activate him.

But as well as filling the gaps in a boring existence, it also had the value of keeping him in trim for times of war, of sharpening his skill in fighting; and it was as such, as a training-ground, that the tournament attained its real position. Rules came to be laid down; the formal challenge was introduced. And wagers were laid; the joust became an important source of revenue to the knight. Provided, of course, he survived. The object of the joust was not the death of the opponent, it was simply an exercise of arms and the knight was made to swear a vow that this was the case before he was allowed to participate. Nonetheless, death was a frequent outcome of the fight, and it was for this reason that tournaments were frowned on by successive kings.

In 1154, Richard I finally recognised them as legal, but under certain conditions. The number of jousting-grounds was limited—only five throughout the country and this did not include Smithfield—and tournaments had to be licensed by the king himself on payment of a fee. It was from this time that the tournament became truly orderly affairs, carried out with pomp and ceremony and the full trappings of heraldry. But there is little doubt that the early tournaments at Smithfield too were colourful events in the life of London.

Norman Remains in Museums

In many categories there are unfortunately few Norman remains to be seen. For example, there is virtually no Norman armour in existence in this country. To get an idea of what it looked like we must turn to contemporary illustrations, in medieval books and manuscripts— for example an 11th century Spanish manuscript in the **British Museum** shows men in armour of the period. But even here the picture is not complete for us since they are shown bearing round shields rather than the kite-shaped shields used in the Conquest. The Bayeux Tapestry provides perhaps the best illustration of the armour worn in the Conquest. However, in the **Wallace Collection,** there is a tiny figure representing an 11th- or 12th-century Norman knight which gives us an example of their armour in three dimension.

The **Wallace Collection** also possesses an excellent collection of European Arms, among which may be seen early medieval swords and axes. Similarly, the **Tower of London** displays swords of the Norman period. These are at present housed in the White Tower, in the Sword Room, but reorganisation is soon to take place and it would be advisable to check on any new arrangements that might have been made. The **Tower** also possesses suits of mail which, if not strictly Norman in period, are roughly similar. There is, too, a conical helmet of Eastern origin which gives an idea of those worn by the Normans.

The Bayeux Tapestry

This Tapestry, made to record the history of the Norman Conquest, was long believed to be the work of William's wife, Matilda, and her ladies, but it is now regarded as more likely the work of English needlewomen, paid for by William's followers in the hope of, or in return for, rewards of land.

Despite its name, the Tapestry is, in fact, more a work of embroidery, coloured stitching on a linen canvas.

Its value to us today, apart from its own intrinsic beauty in colour and design, is the wealth of knowledge it affords us of Norman life. Its 72 'episodes' give us pictures not only of Norman ships, armour, and weapons, the military trappings of the Conquest, but also illustrates the peaceful occupations of the time in town and country life. We have already noted its pictures of cooking. And in the Saxon section of this book we mentioned the Bayeux Tapestry as giving us some idea of what Edward the Confessor's Church at Westminster looked like (illustrated on p. 78).

The original Tapestry is kept at Bayeux in Normandy.

The Domesday Book

The Domesday Book contains the results of the detailed survey of England, undertaken by special officers, on the instructions of William the Conqueror. Its main object was tax assessment.

The task of the Commissioners was to record, shire by shire, 'the name of the manor, who held it in the time of King Edward the Confessor and who held it now, how many hides (an area of about 120 acres) there were in each manor, how many ploughs on the domain, how many men (of all classes), how much wood, how much meadow, how much pasture; what mills, what fish-ponds—how much it was worth and whether more could be got out of it than today.' William also insisted on knowing the details of the livestock: a Saxon chronicler laments: 'It is shameful to record it, but it did not seem shameful for him to do—not even one ox, nor one cow, nor one pig . . . escaped notice in his survey.'

The Book, in two volumes, is still in existence, kept in the Public Record Office in Chancery Lane.

Norman Architecture

The Early Norman Style—Romanesque

The Normans brought with them to this country a new style of architecture—much more ambitious than that of the Saxons—and a zeal for building which led to the construction, between 1066 and 1154, of over seven thousand churches, abbeys, and cathedrals. Most of these were cruciform in plan, and all were characterised by that massiveness and simplicity which is the key-note of early Norman work.

But if they were religious builders, they were secular builders too, and the first task of the Normans was to secure the country by means of castles from invasion or insurrection.

Castles

The first castles built in this country were hastily constructed wooden ones, simple wooden forts set on top of

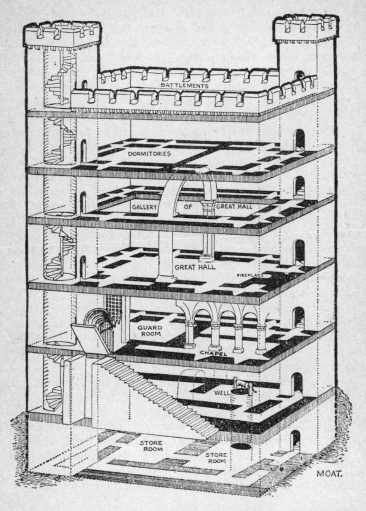

A cross section of a typical Norman keep of the type which was built all over England during the years after the Conquest.

a mound of earth (either natural or artificially raised) and surrounded by a moat and an enclosed yard or 'bailey'—hence the name given to them, 'motte-and-bailey'. The original White Tower of the Tower of London was like this, but by about 1080, in common with other castles throughout the country, the wooden fort was replaced by the stone keep. In some places these keeps were round, but in general they were square.

The characteristic Norman castle, then, had a square tower (high, for purposes of defence against siege) with very thick walls and very narrow windows (again for the same reason). Its purpose was military and defensive; nothing else (comfort or decor) was important. Even the spiral staircase was given a defensive twist—namely, in a clockwise direction from bottom to top so that the defender backing up the stair could protect his body behind the newel post and wield his sword freely against the exposed attacker. The success of this, of course, depended on both attacker and defender conforming to the general rule of being right-handed.

Later developments in castle-building led to greater elaboration—the drawbridges and portcullises, the channels for molten lead we're familiar with from the cinema—but the castle of this period remained basically the simple keep.

Examples of the Norman castle can be seen at Rochester (built about 1126) and at Colchester (built on the site of the Roman Temple to Claudius; larger in area than the White Tower; and now the home of Colchester Museum).

Castle Hedingham in Essex, just off the A132, south of Halstead, is a superb example of the square Norman keep. Built about 1100, it is still in use as a residence.

In London itself, there is, of course, the White Tower.

Religious Buildings
After the initial task of castle-building, the Normans could devote themselves more completely to their re-

ligious buildings. These, rising to dizzy heights, aspiring closer and closer towards Heaven, are the greatest achievements of the Norman architect. There is little doubt that it was the idea of mystical contact with God that made them build so high. It is necessary to understand the fervour of their religious belief; the intensely personal concept of God, revealing himself almost daily in acts of punishment (storms and plagues) and acts of reward (miracles and cures); their superstitions and their fears. Their lives were closely related to (if not dominated by) their religion and their Church. There is no doubt many churches were founded more from fear of God than from adoration. And the inseparability of religious and secular life explains the, to our eyes irrelevent if not downright irreverent, work of the humble mason who carved all sorts of animals and people, frequently in a humorous satirical fashion. This was not irreverence or secularity creeping in where it had no business; it simply meant that to the carver his religion and his craft were one and the same thing. So the immense height of the cathedrals symbolised not only the Church's dominance over the land, but also man's desire to reach Heaven.

Later, architecture was to express these ideas more fully. First, problems posed by them had to be solved.

Early Norman architecture in this country was surprisingly clumsy. Stone-work was crude, and, if the walls were thick, they nonetheless lacked strength. This was because the Normans, unlike the Saxons who had used large blocks of stone, chose to work with smaller stones as an outer casing for their walls and pillars and fill the space inside with rubble.

(This was following the Roman example, as indeed they did in the basic shape of the building which resembled the Roman Basilica—hence the name often applied to this early style of Norman architecture—Romanesque.)

A typical Norman arch showing the lack of ornament

Yet walls had to be strong to support the round arches they wanted to have, so, to achieve this strength, the walls were made thicker than was otherwise necessary. Inferior workmanship, then, was at least part of the reason for the massiveness of structure that is one of the first things that strike us about Norman architecture.

But Norman architects, even in the earliest period, were by no means novices: the main reason for their early crudeness was probably the necessity to use semi-skilled or unskilled Saxon labour. As time went on and the Saxon mason mastered his craft, aided no doubt by an influx of skilled Norman masons, buildings became more polished in conception and finish.

The main characteristics of the Romanesque style, apart from its simple massiveness, are its heavy cylindrical columns and its rounded arches, its contrasting use of circle and square. The square, squat tower is as unmistakably a sign of a Norman church as the vaulted ceilings within.

The development of these ceilings was, to begin with, more a structural necessity than a stylistic device; it was merely their solution to the problem of how to roof over a large space with stone rather than wood, which they had always used before.

The Development of Vaulting

The earliest form of roofing in stone was the simple 'barrel vault'. This created a sort of tunnel effect since it was suitable only for roofing small areas. The first development towards finding a method for larger areas was making two of these barrel vaults intersect at right angles. This was called a 'groined cross-vault', the groin being the angle formed by the line of intersection of the two semi-circular barrel vaults. Ordinary arches across the space were built first, and the cross-vaults built as diagonal supports in the ceiling area between the arches. But this method still didn't provide sufficient strength. It was then found that stronger support was obtained by building the diagonals first.

There then arose problems of elevation and perspective: whether the diagonal ribs of the cross-vault should be semicircular or flatter in shape. And if the space to be covered was oblong in shape rather than square (as in a church aisle) the difficulty was that the arches along the long sides were much higher than those along the short. One solution to this was 'stilting'—heightening the legs of the arch so that the actual curve began higher up the wall. But this effect was ugly and another solution was found, the correct one as it turned out, answering all the problems—the arches across the aisle were to be pointed. The first use of the pointed arch was in Durham Cathedral in 1130, but it did not appear generally until the end of the century.

The evolution of the barrel vault deserves study in far greater detail than the inadequate survey offered here, since it is only by appreciating the difficulties that had to be overcome that we can fully appreciate the intricacy and beauty of the later effects achieved by Norman craftsmen. For example, the incredible fan vaulting of Henry VII's Chapel in Westminster Abbey, though of much later date and in a different style (the 'Perpendicular'), is at bottom a descendant of the humble rib vault.

The Perpendicular period was not, it must be stressed, till some two hundred years later, but a change of style *was* just around the corner for the Normans. The new style was to be called 'Early English', but there was, naturally, an overlap of the old and new; a transitional period.

The Norman Transitional Period

This Norman Transitional period saw a continuation of the early ideas of what church architecture should be (buildings became higher still and even more austere), backed by an increased technical ability. But at the same time it saw the beginning of an Eastern influence, new knowledge of the art of building picked up from contacts made during the Crusades. If the Norman English themselves took little interest in the Holy Wars until Richard the Lion Heart's time, there were many on the continent who did and continental ideas were as easily and speedily imported as continental goods. Thus by about 1170 many features of the new style, first developed in the north of France, were beginning to appear in this country.

This style (which later came to be known as 'Gothic' both on the Continent and in this country) is distinguished by greater elaboration in construction, a new lightness of feeling. It's always difficult to say, in the Transitional period, how many of the new features were taken from abroad, and how many evolved from the advancing technique of the Norman English themselves. Certainly, as we have seen, the pointed arch had been used as early as 1130, and this is one of the major characteristics of the Gothic style. Similarly, stone cutting was vastly improved and the pillars supporting the arches were much thinner than before though supporting greater weight, but whether this developed at home or was learnt abroad we cannot be sure.

However, the important thing is that the changes took place. One of the most vital was the discovery of wall stresses to support the arches. These buttresses meant that the walls could be made thinner at all points except where a thickening was required to support an arch. These passed from being simple ground-level supports for arches to being the main supports of the high ceilings of the buildings. From the main buttress standing on the floor, others were passed at an angle across the gap to connect with the main ceiling vault. This—the use of 'flying buttresses'—is another of the main characteristics of the Early English period. Another is the shape of the windows—tall and thin, with a pointed arch, hence the name 'lancet' windows.

The earlier Norman windows had been much squatter —simply small holes, topped by round arches, often a series of them getting smaller the nearer they were to the wall. The door was of similar design, decorated with all sorts of carvings, both abstract designs and the representations of animals and men we mentioned before. The carvings were simple because the tools the craftsman had were not suitable for anything more adventurous—the usual tool would have been a pick or an axe.

By the Early English period the chisel was re-introduced for the first time since the Romans. Consequently the art of the carver could improve. The change can be seen especially in the decoration of the columns and the capitals at their heads. Whereas the Norman columns had been ornamented with thinly cut patterns (usually spirals or zig-zags, also called 'chevrons') the Early English carver used his chisel to undercut and bring the decorations out farther from the stone. For much the same sort of effect, to achieve an outward movement, the columns themselves came to be surrounded with separate shafts of stone.

All these changes took place over a long period of time and the new features were not all in general usage until well into the 13th century.

Monasteries

The part played by the monasteries in Norman society as a whole was an important one; the part played by them in architecture was indispensable. For one thing, the amount of land they owned was considerable (almost a fifth of the country); for another, through their endowments they were able to finance building on a large scale. They were, too, the centres of learning, and as such they had the fullest knowledge of architecture, its history, and its latest developments.

A monastery itself consisted of church, cloisters, chapter house, sacristy, and monks' quarters. The size of the establishment can be gathered from the fact that a cathedral as we now know it was often only the actual church, just one of the many monastic buildings.

Monks played an active part in secular as well as religious life. Abbots were great men, working close to the king; ordinary monks were the teachers and social workers of their day. They were also inn-keepers; country inns were few and far between at this time, and it was part of the duty of the monks to provide hospitality for travellers.

Hospitality—hospital: the words have the same origin —from the Latin 'hospes', meaning a guest. Only later did a hospital become a place for the sick alone. The first hospitals in this country were founded at this time—St. Bartholomew's Hospital dates from 1123, St. Thomas's from 1173.

Another offshoot of the monastery was the university. By the time it had become university in name it had severed all direct contact with the monastery, but the fact remains that the earliest university evolved from the cloister schools where the monks taught. Although Oxford had no actual university building till the 15th century, its origins can be seen in the 12th century when a group of students from the already established University of Paris settled there in 1167. Not long afterwards some of the Oxford group migrated to Cambridge.

In the 12th century many new Orders of monks were formed, including the White Friars, whose monastery in London is commemorated in Whitefriars Street, which runs from Fleet Street to the Embankment. And one of the Crusading Orders, the Knights Templar, established themselves in this country with headquarters at the Temple.

Norman Buildings in London

St. Bartholomew the Great

There is a legend surrounding the foundation of this church, the oldest surviving in London.

Rahere, a courtier at the time of Henry I, went on a pilgrimage to Rome. He became sick and in a delirium saw himself being suspended over Hell by a fiend. He was so troubled by this vision that he swore that if he was allowed to recover he would build a hospital. St. Bartholomew then appeared to him, and, as a result Rahere vowed to build as well a great Priory Church in his honour. He recovered completely and on his return to England, Rahere became a monk and later founded both the Priory and the Hospital in 1123.

That is the legend, and it offers a perfect illustration of the Norman Christian mind at work—the visualisation of Demon and Saint; the fear of Hell and Damnation inspiring the foundation of a church to God. But the important

thing was the founding of the church and the good work
it did, whatever caused it to be built. As we have seen,
Rahere made a good Prior, using the proceeds of his fair
to endow both Priory and Hospital.

The legend is told pictorially on panels at the back of
the church, whose massive columns and rounded arches
offer us a perfect example of the Romanesque style of
architecture.

Further details on St. Bartholomew's will be found
later in a suggested walk.

St. Mary-Le-Bow

This church in Cheapside is more famous for its Bow
Bells than for any Norman connections. Nevertheless, it
stands above an early Norman crypt—late 11th century
in fact, and therefore of an earlier date than St. Bartholomew's, but unfortunately the crypt is all that has
survived. The name, 'le-Bow' seems to have derived from
the medieval name 'St. Maria-de-Arcubus'—'arcus' means
an 'arch' or 'bow', and the church, built on stone arches
(i.e. the crypt), was given this nick-name in honour of
being the first in London to be so built. The crypt, part
of it restored, again offers a glimpse of the massive
columns of early Norman work.

The entrance to the crypt is on the outside of the
building, on the south-west side.

St. John's Priory, Clerkenwell

The Order of the Hospital of St. John of Jerusalem, or
more simply, the Knights Hospitaller, was founded in
Jerusalem about 1100. Its aim was to protect pilgrims to
the Holy Land. About forty years later the order founded
a Priory in Clerkenwell on the site of the present church.
Again all that remains of the original building is the
crypt, another example of mid-12th century Norman
work—mature Norman rather than Transitional.

The only other reminder of the original church still to

be seen is the outline of its nave in St. John's Square. This was unusual in that it was round; but a round nave tended to be the rule rather than the exception in the churches of the Crusading Orders—for a reason we shall see when we come to the Temple.

Further details on St. John's will be found later in a suggested walk.

The Temple Church

Within the Temple, just to the north of Inner Temple Hall is the Temple Church, consecrated in 1185.

The Order of the Knights Templar, another of the Crusading Orders, was founded in Jerusalem in 1119. Their original London base was in Holborn. In 1160 they moved to the Temple. The Order lasted until 1312 when it was suppressed by the Pope. The Temple properties were then passed to the Knights Hospitaller who remained in existence (as in fact they are today), and they began to lease them out to professors of law. This is the origin of the Temple's legal associations.

The Temple Church can be looked on as an excellent example of Norman Transitional, offering as it does a nave in Norman style and a chancel in Early English.

The nave is round (as that of St. John's had been), and the reason for this is that it was modelled on the Church of the Holy Sepulchre in Jerusalem. Part of the aim of the Crusading Orders was the protection of the Holy Sepulchre from the Mohammedans, so it is understandable that its circular shape should be adopted by these Orders when they came to build their own churches. On the floor may be seen effigies of Knights of the Order, first made in the 12th and 13th centuries and now restored after bomb damage in the last war; and on the capitals of the columns round the wall are carved faces, many of them grotesque—an example of the seemingly secular work of the Norman mason which we discussed in the section on Religious Building.

The chancel is of later date, 1240, and therefore offers us some examples of fairly well-developed Early English work. Here we can see, for instance, the lancet windows, grouped in threes, and also, overhead, an example of fan-vaulting.

The church was in fact badly hit by bombing during the last war, and much of what can be seen is restoration; but restoration so careful and so close to the original as to be indistinguishable.

The White Tower of the Tower of London

The White Tower is, as we have already noted, the oldest part of the Tower of London. The architect, Gundolph (later to become Bishop of Rochester), began the replacement of the old wooden motte-and-bailey by this stone keep in about 1078. The other buildings which now make up the Tower of London were added later: the inner wall with its thirteen towers in the middle of the 13th century, the outer wall with the six towers on the river side later the same century. The towers on the north came much later still, in the reign of Henry VIII.

The White Tower is rectangular, about 118 feet by 107, has four stories with walls varying in thickness from 11 to 15 feet, and stands about 90 feet high. The original approach to the White Tower was on the south side, but today the entrance is on the north, by an outside staircase.

The most interesting part of the White Tower from the point of view of Norman times is the Chapel of St. John. This is on the second floor, reached by way of a staircase from the Small Arms Room on the western half of the first floor, (the south end of which contains the Crypt of the Chapel, now used to display instruments of torture).

St. John's Chapel is the oldest example of Norman religious architecture, older even than St. Bartholomew the Great at Smithfield. Here we can see the characteristic arches and pillars of the nave, and also over the clerestory, the simple barrel vault. And here too we can see an example of stilting, in the five stilted arches connecting the apse to an ambulatory.

The White Tower must have been a most forbidding place to the citizens of Norman London, and even to those who lived there it cannot have afforded much pleasure or comfort. Today the White Tower retains its medieval atmosphere and a visit to it will convey better than any words could what it must have been like living in a Norman castle.

Buildings in London with Norman Remains or Associations

Southwark Cathedral

As was noted in the Saxon section, the original church on the site of Southwark Cathedral was taken over in the 9th century by a college of priests. In 1106, this college, established by St. Swithin of Winchester, was itself absorbed into an Augustine priory. The Augustines built

The two sides of a coin of Henry II, the great law giver

a great Norman church, which was burned down a century later in 1206, and was replaced by London's first pure Gothic-style cathedral.

There are still some traces of the Norman church in the present Cathedral. Through the door to the vestry (which can be visited) there are remains of a Norman arch; the north transept is Norman, as are the arches to the Harvard Chapel (John Harvard was the founder of the famous American University); and in the north choir aisle there is a wooden effigy of a crusading knight.

Southwark was for long in the diocese of Winchester (in fact, until 1877)—hence the street names, Winchester Walk and Winchester Square. In the present cathedral there is a model of the old church and Palace of the Bishops of Winchester.

To this we may add **Westminster Hall,** whose Norman associations have been mentioned in the main text and **Westminster Abbey,** whose associations have been covered in the Saxon section (the Cloisters and the Chamber of the Pyx, all that remain of the Confessor's Norman-style church).

A walk around Smithfield

St. Bartholomew's is on the east side of Smithfield. The entrance is through an arch beside a small restaurant, under a timbered Gatehouse built in 1595, but much restored.

Walk through the arch towards the church. The path goes through the burial ground which now covers the area once occupied by the nave of the church before the Dissolution of the Monasteries at the time of Henry VIII. On the right there are the bases of the old columns which originally supported the roof of the south aisle. Over the door in the entrance porch is a figure representing the founder of the Priory, Rahere, who holds a model of the church in his hand.

The present church is all that is left of a great Priory Church and is actually only the choir and transepts of the original, plus the Lady Chapel which was built in

1336. Built in 1123, it is the oldest surviving church in the City and is a fine example of Norman architecture.

The tomb of Rahere lies to the left of the altar which is surrounded by Rahere's simple rounded arches. Above these is the clerestory, rebuilt in the early 15th century, and to the right is an oriel window erected by Prior Bolton about 1520. On the front of the window is a rebus, or sign, representing the syllables of his name—a crossbow bolt through a cask or tun—Bolt-in-ton, from which his name derives.

At the back of the church are some painted panels representing parts of the legend of Rahere.

The Lady Chapel was used for many purposes, including a dwelling house, a workshop for a printer, in which the American Benjamin Franklin worked for a time, and a fringe-factory.

St. John's Priory

Leave St. Bartholomew's and turn right. Walk straight through the main arch in the middle of Smithfield market and straight on to St. John Street. Bear left up St. John's Lane to the Gatehouse of the Priory of St. John of Jerusalem.

The Knights Hospitaller were founded in the early 12th century to protect pilgrims to the Holy Land, and the English branch founded a Priory in Clerkenwell. The Priory was abolished at the time of the Dissolution and the Gatehouse, built in 1504, is all that remains from this early foundation. The Museum in the Gatehouse is open to visitors on application.

The church of the priory has been rebuilt many times, including after the last war, but the crypt is still original and is one of the few examples of early 12th-century architecture remaining in London.

To get to it from St. John's Gate, cross Clerkenwell Road, to St. John's Square, and the entrance to the church is on the right. Another reminder of the Knights of St.

John of Jerusalem is the alley, Jerusalem Passage, which leads northwards out of the square.

Not Norman, but nearby:
Charterhouse, in Charterhouse Square—open to visitors at 2.45 p.m. on Wednesdays, April to July (fee 4s 9d). From Smithfield, walk through the market area and turn right.

Nearest Underground: Aldersgate, on Metropolitan Line—out of station, turn right along Long Lane to Smithfield.

Bus: to High Holborn Railway Station—walk up Giltspur Street.

Norman Buildings Outside London
Waltham Abbey
Waltham Abbey, traditionally the burial site of King Harold, offers in particular splendid examples of round piers with spiral and chevron groovings.

Rochester Cathedral
Built by Bishop Gundolph, the architect of the White Tower, has Norman work surviving in the nave, aisles, and crypt, again showing the characteristic zig-zag, etc.

St. Alban's Cathedral
In this Cathedral (begun in 1077) most of the usual Norman features can again be seen, but perhaps the most interesting because rare are the paintings (of an early medieval date) on the solid Norman piers in the north arcade of the nave.

The Church of St. Mary Magdalene, East Ham
This church in East Ham, within easy reach of London (in fact on the Metropolitan and District Lines of the

Underground) was built about 1130 and remains remarkably unspoilt. Here again you can see the rounded Norman windows in the chancel and a large Norman arch between the chancel and the nave. But there are rarer things to look out for. The timbers in the roof of the chancel are original, and on its north wall is a rare example of 'blind' arcading (with the remains of some on the south wall).

You may notice, above the arch dividing the chancel from the nave, a bricked-up arch—this was the entrance to what used to be a loft over the chancel. On the north wall of the chancel is a small slit window which was placed there to afford a view of the altar from the cell on the other side of the window. This cell, now blocked off by an outside door, was used by an anchorite—a hermit. A skeleton discovered some time ago when digging was in progress to clear the ground round the church was thought to be that of an anchorite.

The original doorway to the church is under the tower, and, being enclosed in the porch, is in a remarkable state of preservation.

The Church of St. Mary Magdalene is on the corner of Norman Road and South Street, just off Beckton Road, E.6.

To these we may add Barking Abbey, whose Norman associations have been noted in the Saxon section.

How to Get There

Guy's Hospital

Address: St. Thomas Street,
S.E.1.

By Underground:

London Bridge Station (Northern Line, Via Bank)—come out of station on to Borough High Street and turn left into St. Thomas Street: the hospital is on the right hand side of the street.

By Bus:

7, 8a, 10, 13, 21, 35, 40, 43, 47, 133 and 257 across London Bridge—get off for London Bridge Station and turn into St. Thomas Street.

The shelter from the old London Bridge is in one of the quadrangles of the Hospital—visitors are usually admitted to it.

Southwark Cathedral

Address: London Bridge, S.E.1.

By Underground and by Bus:

As for Guy's Hospital.

The Cathedral is on the West side of Borough High Street, almost directly opposite London Bridge Station.

It is suggested that a visit to Guy's Hospital and a visit to Southwark Cathedral might be combined into one outing. And note Tooley Street, which adjoins Borough High Street on the east side, just to the north of the station.

All Hallows Berkynge by the Tower

Address: Byward Street, E.C.3.

By Underground:

Tower Hill (Circle and District Lines)—turn left out of station down path to Byward Street. Turn right along Byward Street. All Hallows is opposite, in the angle between Byward Street and Great Tower Street.

By Bus:

Nearest bus routes are the 42 and 78 in the Minories—get off at Tower Bridge and walk along above the Tower to All Hallows; or the 10 and 70 in Fenchurch Street —get off for Mark Lane and walk down Lane to Great Tower Street. Slightly farther away are the buses which cross London Bridge, the 7, 8a, 10, 13, 21, 35, 40, 43, 47, 133 and 257—get off at north side of Bridge and walk to the east through Lower Thames Street, past Billingsgate Market and turning north just past Custom House.

The Tower of London
Address: Tower Hill, E.C.3.
By Underground and Bus:
As for All Hallows Berkynge by the Tower.
Tower Hill, the open space to the west of the Tower
faces you as you turn left out of the station.
It is suggested that a visit to the Tower and a visit to All
Hallows might be combined into one outing.

The Temple Church
Address: Fleet Street, E.C.4.
By Underground:
Temple Station (Circle and District)—turn left out of
station and head north to the Strand. Turn right on the
Strand and continue till it joins Fleet Street at Temple
Bar. (Note in passing St. Clement Danes Church on your
left in the Strand.) Continue along Fleet Street to Inner
Temple Lane, turn right into Lane through the gateway,
and follow lane to Church.
Chancery Lane (Central Line)—turn into Chancery Lane
and continue till it joins Fleet Street. Gateway to Inner
Temple Lane is directly opposite. (NB: Chancery Lane
Station is closed on a Sunday. Also, Aldwych Station,
possibly the nearest—turn right out of station, along
Strand and Fleet Street to Inner Temple Lane—is open
only at rush hours.)
By Bus:
4a, 6, 9, 11, 13 and 15 run along Fleet Street—get off for
Inner Temple Lane.
109, 177 and 184 run along Victoria Embankment—get
off for Temple.
7, 8, 22, 23 and 25 run along High Holborn—get off for
Chancery Lane.

St. Bride's Church
Address: Fleet Street, E.C.4.

By Underground:

Blackfriars Station (Circle and District; and Southern Region)—turn north along New Bridge Street to Ludgate Circus (with St. Paul's Cathedral up Ludgate Hill on your right). Turn left at Ludgate Circus into Fleet Street: the entrance to St. Bride's Church is on your left, beside the Reuters building.

By Bus:

17, 45, 63, 76, 109, 141, 177 and 184 run across Blackfriars Bridge—get off for Blackfriars or (on 17, 45, 63, 141, plus the 168) at Ludgate Circus. Otherwise, as for The Temple Church—the two churches might be visited on one outing.

St. Bartholomew The Great (Smithfield)

By Underground:

Aldersgate (Metropolitan and Circle). (NB: This station is not open on Sundays.)
Farringdon (Metropolitan and Circle).
St. Paul's (Central).

By Bus:

7, 8, 22, 23 and 25 run along Holborn Viaduct—get off for Giltspur Street.
63, 143 and 221 run along Farringdon Road—get off for Holborn Viaduct (Charterhouse Street or Long Lane).
4a runs along Aldersgate Street—get off for Long Lane.

St. John's Church (Clerkenwell)

By Underground:

Farringdon (Metropolitan and Circle).
Aldersgate (Metropolitan and Circle—Not open on Sundays).

By Bus:

5, 170 run along Clerkenwell Road—get off to west of junction with John Street.

63, 143 and 221 run along Farringdon Road—get off for Clerkenwell Road.
4 and 277 run along Goswell Road.
279 runs along St. John Street.
NB. For further details on St. Bartholomew's and St. John's, see suggested walk.

St. Mary-Le-Bow

Address: Cheapside, E.C.2

By Underground:
St. Paul's (Central Line)—from station walk along Cheapside—Church is on the right, just before the junction of Cheapside and Queen Street.
Bank (Central and Northern Line)—from station walk along Poultry until it becomes Cheapside: the church is on the left, just after junction of Cheapside and Queen Street.
Mansion House (Circle and District)—from station follow Queen Victoria Street across Cannon Street till it joins Queen Street; turn left into Queen Street, then left again at junction with Cheapside.

By Bus:
7, 8, 22, 23 and 25 run along Poultry and Cheapside.
4 (4a) runs along Aldersgate Street—get off for St. Paul's, walk along Cheapside.

Westminster Abbey (S.W.1)

By Underground:
Westminster (Circle and District)—turn right out of station on Bridge Street and cross square.
St. James's Park (Circle and District)—turn right out of station and walk straight on for Abbey.

By Bus:
3, 11, 24, 29, 39, 59, 76, 77, 88, 127, 134, 159, 163, and 168.

Opening Hours:

    Daily: 8 am—7 pm (6 pm October—March)

    (On Sundays only the nave and transepts open)

Chamber of the Pyx:

    Weekdays: 10.30 am—6.30 pm (4 pm in winter)

    Admission free

Norman Undercroft (Abbey Museum):

    Weekdays: 10.30 am—4.30 pm (4 pm in winter)

    Admission 6d

The main entrance to the Abbey is by the West Door, but access to the Chamber of the Pyx and the Norman Undercroft can be gained from Dean's Yard by the South Cloister.

Glossary of Architectural Terms

Arcade: a sequence of arches on columns. (Blind arcade: where some of the arches are filled in)

Buttress: a vertical wall stress of masonry, projecting from the wall. (Flying Buttress) arched masonry, passing the weight of roof-vaulting on to wall buttresses.

Capital: the top of a column (or pillar), frequently carved.

Chevron: (Or Zig-zag) the name given to a thinly-cut zig-zag pattern on columns and capitals.

Lancet Window:	a tall narrow window with a pointed head (like the head of a lance).
Stilted Arch:	an arch whose curve begins well above the capital, which is normally the starting-off point of the arch.
Vault:	an arched covering in stone. **Barrel-vault:** a simple arched roofing in stone, tunnel-like since unbroken by cross-vaults. **Groined Cross-vault:** the inter-section at right angles of two barrel-vaults.

Parts of a Church

Aisle:	lateral division of a church separated from nave, transept or choir by pillars.
Ambulatory:	the aisle round an apse or across the eastern end of a church.
Apse:	an arched recess at the end of a church; a side chapel.
Chancel:	the eastern part of a church.
Choir:	part of a church set aside for the choir and the clergy.
Cruciform:	in the shape of a cross.
Crypt:	the vault under a church.
Nave:	the main body of a church.
Transept:	the transverse part of a cruciform church, either arm.

Norman Art

As has been suggested in the main text, art in the Norman period was closely bound up with religion; connected to, if not inseparable from, the Church. Artist and craftsman alike dedicated themselves to the creation of religious art, and we are fortunate enough to possess many examples of this.

In the **Victoria and Albert Museum**, for example, Room 43, just through from the main entrance, houses a collection of Early Medieval Art, amongst which may be seen several superb examples of English craftsmanship in the Romanesque style of the 11th and 12th centuries, many of them carvings in bone and whalebone—for example a relief in whalebone of the Adoration of the Magi. Other exhibits to look out for are the Gloucester Candlestick of about 1110; the Narwhal Horn (carved with grotesque animals etc., probably part of a ceremonial staff) from the second quarter of the 12th century; two initials from a Manuscript of St. Gregory on Job; and a leaf from a Psalter from between 1130 and 1150.

(In the same room can be seen some Saxon work—a sandstone cross of the 9th century and crosses in walrus ivory, for example.)

In the **London Museum**, a more general collection of Norman remains can be seen, including a leather sheaf (decorated with scrolls round birds) from 12th century Westminster; keys from London (pre-Conquest, but in a form which continued in use during the 11th and 12th centuries); a cresset lamp made from a 12th-century capital (found on the site of the G.P.O.); various knives; a decorated bowl of the 12th century; and an oval stirrup found in Lothbury. There is also a case which contains a map of the sitings of medieval buildings in the City, Westminster, and Southwark, with photographs of many of them. There are too, models of Old St. Paul's and of

London Bridge, about 1600, which, though not strictly Norman, have Norman associations.

Guildhall Museum displays, for example, some bone chessmen of the 12th and 13th centuries, and arrow heads of the same period, as well as a cooking pot with handles and spout, and a portion of a stone figure (probably a bishop) from the 12th century. There is also in the Guildhall an interesting map of North-West Europe showing the change in trade routes from Saxon times to the Middle Ages.

Visits to these museums, as indeed to the **Victoria and Albert,** should probably be made with a view to combining both Saxon and Norman remains at the same time.

The same may be said of the **British Museum,** whose **King Edward VII Gallery** at the back of the building (which can be entered from Montague Place) houses a comprehensive collection of British and Medieval Antiquities, which includes both Saxon (the Sutton Hoo Treasure, for example, as well as much late Saxon metal work) and Norman remains. Amongst the latter may be noted the Lewis Chessmen of the 12th century (Romanesque in style, carved in Walrus Ivory); a Romanesque portable altar; other Romanesque work, of the 11th to 13th centuries; a bronze bowl, engraved, of the 12th; and later medieval pottery of the 13th and 14th centuries.

Also in the **British Museum,** of interest to this period, is the **Manuscript Room,** already noted in the Saxon section, where in addition to the Lindisfarne Gospels, and the works of Bede, previously mentioned, many medieval charters and illuminated manuscripts can be seen.

APPENDIX 'A'

MUSEUM LIST
LONDON MUSEUM

Address:

Kensington Palace,
Kensington Gardens, W.8

Admission:

Free

Opening hours:

1 March—30 September:
10 am—6 pm (Sundays: 2 pm—6 pm)
1 October—28 February:
10 am—4 pm (Sundays: 2pm—4 pm)

Closed:

Good Friday, Christmas Eve, and
Christmas Day

Access:

By Underground:

Queensway (Central Line)—cross Bayswater Road and walk through Broad Walk in Kensington Gardens to Palace.
Kensington High Street (Circle & District Line from Earls Court to Edgware Road)—turn right along Kensington High Street to Park. Left through Park to Palace.

By Bus:

12, 88, along Bayswater Road to Queensway, then as above from Queensway Station.
9, 46, 52, 73, to Palace Gate in Kensington Road. Walk through Park to Palace.

By Car:

The best place to park is in the squares and side streets off Bayswater Road or Kensington Road. Then walk through Park.

BRITISH MUSEUM

Address:

Great Russell Street, W.C.1

Admission:

Free

Opening hours:

Monday—Saturday: 10 am—5pm
Sunday: 2.30 pm—6 pm

Closed:

Christmas Day and Good Friday.
Open Bank Holidays usual hours

Access:

By Underground:

Tottenham Court Road (Central & Northern Lines)—turn right along Tottenham Court Road and right at Great Russell Street. Museum on left.

Russell Square (Piccadilly Line)—left out of station, cross Russell Square, and left on Montague Street to Great Russell Street and main entrance of Museum.

By Bus:

77, 68, 188, 196, to Southampton Row. Turn left along Great Russell Street.

73 to Tottenham Court Road/Oxford Street. Right along Great Russell Street.

7, 8, 23, 25, to Bloomsbury Way. Turn along Museum Street (from West).

7, 8, 22, 23, 25, from Holborn direction. Alight at High Holborn, just past Kingsway, and cross road, along Drury Lane or Grape Street, cross New Oxford Street and continue along Coptic Street or Museum Street.

By Car:

Drive from West along Oxford Street, turn left at Tottenham Court Road, and right almost immediately at Great Russell Street.

From East, along Holborn to Kingsway, turn right along Southampton Row, and left at Great Russell Street. N.B. There is limited parking at the Museum—otherwise, at side in Montague Street/Russell Square.

GUILDHALL MUSEUM

Address:

> On Bassishaw High Walk, up stairs by Gillette House in Basinghall Street, overlooking London Wall, E.C.2

Admission:

> Free

Opening hours:

> Monday—Saturday: 10 am—5pm

Closed:

> Sundays, Bank Holidays, Holy Days— e.g. Christmas and Good Friday

Access:

By Underground:

Aldersgate (Metropolitan or Circle Lines)—turn right out of station along Aldersgate as far as London Wall. Turn left—Museum up on high walk-way opposite ruin of church tower.

St. Paul's (Central Line)—walk along Cheapside to Wood Street, left to Gresham Street, right for one block to Aldermanbury. Up stairs on right at end before junction with London Wall.

Moorgate (Metropolitan & Northern Lines)—turn right along Moorgate, to London Wall. Turn right.

Bank (Central Line)—along Princes Street at side of Bank of England to Gresham Street. Left as far as Basinghall Street. Right. Museum at far end of Basinghall Street up steps by Gillette House.

By Bus:

7, 8, 22, 23, 25, to St. Paul's end of Cheapside, then follow instructions given under St. Paul's Underground Station above.

76, 43, 21, 11, 9, 141, to London Wall/Moorgate. Follow instructions as from Moorgate Station.

By Car:

Parking is difficult except at weekends out of 'meter' hours. No parking at any time on London Wall.

From East: drive to the Bank then along Princes Street by Bank of England, turn left at Gresham Street, and right at Aldermanbury.

From West: Holborn/Newgate Street, turn left at Aldersgate and right at Gresham Street. Park in area behind Guildhall.

CUMING MUSEUM

Address:

Above Library next to Town Hall, Walworth Road, Southwark S.E.17

Admission:

Free

Opening Hours:

Opens Monday—Saturday: 10 am
Closes at 5.30 pm except Thursday at 7 pm. Saturday at 5 pm

Closed:

Sundays, Bank Holidays, and Holy Days

Access:

By Underground:

Elephant & Castle (Bakerloo & Northern Lines)—out of station, cross Newington Butts, bear right, round traffic circuits to Walworth Road on left. About 300 yards along on left.

By Bus:
12, 17, 35, 40A, 45, to Museum. Ask for Town Hall, Walworth Road.

By Car:
Aim at Elephant and Castle which is well signposted. Drive round traffic circuit and bear left at Walworth Road, direction Camberwell. Museum on left about 300 yards along. Park in side streets.

VICTORIA AND ALBERT MUSEUM
Address:

South Kensington, S.W.7

Admission:

Free

Opening hours:

Monday—Saturday: 10 am—6 pm
Sunday: 2.30 pm—6 pm

Closed:

Christmas Day and Good Friday
Open Bank Holidays usual hours

Access:

By Underground:
South Kensington (District, Circle and Piccadilly Lines)—a subway connects the station and the museum, giving entrance on N.W. (Exhibition Road) side. Main entrance to museum is on Cromwell Road.

By Bus:
207, 45, 49, to South Kensington Station.
14, 30, 74, to Brompton Oratory, at junction of Brompton Road and Cromwell Road.

WALLACE COLLECTION
Address:

Hertford House, Manchester Square, W.1

Admission:

Free

Opening hours:

> Monday—Saturday: 10 am—5 pm
> Sunday: 2 pm—5 pm

Closed:

> Good Friday, Christmas Eve and Christmas Day

Access:

By Underground:
Bond Street (Central Line)—turn left out of station along Oxford Street until junction with Duke Street. Cross Oxford Street and continue N. along Duke Street, crossing Wigmore Street, till Duke Street opens on to Manchester Square. The Wallace Collection is on the far (N.) side of the square.

Baker Street (Bakerloo, Circle, and Metropolitan Lines)—cross Marylebone Road and walk down Baker Street as far as George Street, turn left into George Street: rear of Hertford House is on the right.

By Bus:
2, 13, 23, 30, 59, 74, 113, 159 run along Baker Street (southbound) and Gloucester Place (northbound)—get off at George Street and walk through to Collection. (Or, as 59 and 159 run along Wigmore Street, get off there for Duke Street.)

6, 7, 8, 12, 13, 15, 23, 60, 73, 88, 113, 137, run along Oxford Street—get off at Selfridges, and walk up Duke Street to the Collection.

Further reading list

Arthur B. Allen	*Norman England to 1154: The Background Book,* The Rockliff New Project Series, Barrie & Rockliff
Peter Hunter Blair	*Roman Britain and Early England,* A History of England (vol i), Thomas Nelson

Christopher Brooke	*From Alfred to Henry III*, A History of England (vol ii), Thomas Nelson
Arthur Bryant	*The Story of England: Makers of the Realm*, Collins
John Finnemore	*Social Life in England: 1—From the Early English to the Middle Ages*, A. & C. Black
Henry Loyn & Alan Sorrell	*Norman Britain*, Lutterworth Press
John Penoyre & Michael Ryan	*The Observer's Book of Architecture*, Frederick Warne
Marjorie & C. H. B. Quennell	*Everyday Life in Roman and Anglo-Saxon Times*, Batsford
Marjorie & C. H. B. Quennell	*A History of Everyday Things in England from 1066–1499*, Batsford
R. R. Sellman	*The Anglo-Saxons*, Methuen
Sir Frank Stenton	*Anglo-Saxon England*, The Oxford History of England, Clarendon Press
Dorothy Whitelock	*The Beginnings of English Society*, Pelican History of England, Penguin
E. L. Woodward	*History of England*, University Paperbacks, Methuen